DIAMOND Jubilee

QUEEN ELIZABETH II

EDITED BY DONNA SAMWORTH

forward poetry

First published in Great Britain in 2012 by:
Forward Poetry
Remus House
Coltsfoot Drive
Peterborough
PE2 9BF
Telephone: 01733 890099
Website: www.forwardpoetry.co.uk

FOREWORD

Here at Forward Poetry our aim has
always been to provide a bridge to publication for
unknown poets and allow their work to reach a wider
audience. We believe that poetry should not be exclusive or
elitist but available to be accessed and appreciated by all.

We are proud to present our latest anthology,
Diamond Jubilee, inspired by the 60-year reign of
Her Majesty Queen Elizabeth II. In June 2012 the whole
country came together in celebration of the Jubilee and
inspired hundreds of poets to join in the celebrations
using their skill with the written word.

With poetry from an assortment of voices and in
a variety of styles, this warm and touching anthology
shows the love and respect the British public have for
the Queen, which made the selection process
an enjoyable and rewarding experience.

CONTENTS

THE POEMS

A Royal Day

I turned my head to look at her, still sound asleep,
got from the bed so quietly, then heard the bleep –
alarm clock noises start the day with their loud shout,
another busy day ahead without a doubt!

I had my constitutional, breakfast next,
but still my lady was not down. I felt quite vexed,
until she came and cuddled me, then all was well!
Today would be a special one, this I could tell.

She wore the sparkling jewels that gleamed
and caught the light,
I felt so proud to own her smile, so warm and bright.
The hours went by and people cheered. I heard the noise
as men and women joined the throng and girls and boys.

Then horses clipped their prancing way along the road.
Now drawing nearer, bringing back their special load.
The carriage rattled through the gates – she has returned!
Another celebration done! A good rest earned!

I cannot wait to have her here, all on my own,
with time to gaze into my eyes, forget the throne
and sit with me and stroke my back, fondle my ears,
then I will give a Corgi lick to calm her fears.

Doris Townsend

The Diamond Jubilee

Sixty years on the throne
Oh, how much the country has grown
She is the ruler of our nation
At 25 she had her coronation

She's had her Silver and her Gold
The country will come together
To have a party which will last forever

She has a crown
But never a frown
The Queen's smile
It would last for a mile.

Liam Pring

The Queen's Diamond Jubilee

I'm busy at the sewing machine, making all the bunting flags to tie at the table to celebrate the day
The sandwiches are all made, the home-made jellies in the dish and lemonade and the ginger fizz.
We, all outside, watching the parade on TV, all exited, wishing it was me.
Don't they all look lovely as we watch the crowds go wild and we tuck into the
 homemade spread.
We celebrate on our street, the children wearing their Jubilee hats and waving their homemade flags as we sit and relax.
The weather really sunny, we've got plenty of time to eat more and enjoy the company of friends that all join us on time.
Pots of tea and crisps and bread and butter that's in a dish, home-made buns and cakes that taste so good, This how we should celebrate this on a lovely, special day.
Oh look, they are in the front now, in the carriages, Her Majesty waving with a beautiful smile on her face and Charles – and look at Kate, such a pretty girl.
But sadly it finishes too quickly, but ah, we can watch it all over again as I've left the video on to watch it at nine.

Amanda Renyard

JUBILEE
(HAWICK JUBILEE PARTY – ARTBEAT STYLE)

Hawick Jubilee Party – Artbeat Style
Jim and I set off by taxi at half-past eleven,
When we went in we were in seventh HEAVEN,
Artbeat had prepared for us a lovely spread,
Sultana scones and gingerbread,
Tray bakes,
Lots of cakes,
Sausages on a stick,
Eat your fill,
Take your pick,
Three cheers,
No tears,
A few beers,
The children all were excited,
The adults were all delighted,
To see our dear Queen
On a large, cinema screen,
I have to hand it to Artbeat they did it with style
And everybody wore a smile,
We all got a souvenir,
So we could remember Jubilee Year,
Bunting on the wall,
Union Jacks waving in the hall,
Everyone happy and all
I recall,
Watching the Queen when I was small,
To me
She was what a Queen should be
And now we've seen her Diamond Jubilee,
So lads and lassies,
Raise your glasses
Long Live Elizabeth
Long Live Elizabeth
Long Live Elizabeth
I'm glad I came
And so did Blind Jim in whose company I was with.

ALAN POW

SILVER, GOLD, DIAMOND LUXURY

It is the year of the diamond
A simple element of carbon
The basis of life
Which, under the right conditions
Turned magnificent
Became the most desired

A symbol of:
Love
Money
Age
Success

And so it had rightly been achieved
It mat be said
As the Queen
Has not lost her head

She has stuck to her guns
To the British Roots
And on that note I bid you adieu.

SUSANNAH ROOKE

JUBILEE CAKE

One day I'll bake a cake;
With icing on top sifted with sugar!
All arranged in decorative order.
To please a poet and lady of renown,
Resting upon layers of finery and scrolls
There will stand a man and lady of celebration,
So happy as man and wife before the nation!
This cake, once baked, will be presented with red carnation!

CHRISTINE FLOWERS

London, Summer 2012

London, summer twenty twelve
Is the only place to be,
We're hosting the Olympics
And the Royal Jubilee.
The athletes practice and perfect
In time for their big day,
But the Queen is up and ready
And already on her way.

The golden Gloriana leads
A thousand-boat flotilla,
A million line the Thames
To watch the pageant down the river;
From Battersea to Tower Bridge,
Historical event,
To mark the jubilation on
A four-day long weekend.

There's people dancing in the street,
There's multi-ethnic food to eat,
And British folk of every hue
Proudly wave red, white and blue;
United for this rare occasion,
Come together as a nation,
Sending up a roar of cheers,
Honouring those sixty years.

Elizabeth, our sovereign queen,
How strong and steadfast you have been;
A diamond monarch through and through,
And we, the people, thank you.

Janet Greenwood

ROYAL ANGST

It's harder than it looks
Being regal
Standing up for hours
Plastic smiles
Do this –
Don't do that!

You can't sign anything unofficial
Not even a school friend's cast
You can't go out
Without a bodyguard
Like a prison

You're under-appreciated
By the masses
Whilst sat at home
The whole world passes

You do what you can, but -
It's never enough
You just have to bear it
Sit down and be tough

A life that is normal
As normal could be
You can dream I suppose
It just won't be

I could not fathom
The things that you've seen
Or done for us all
Fair lady
Our Queen.

DAT GUY DERE

DIAMOND DAY

June's England! Raindrops glisten from the boughs
of overhanging trees, where damp birds drowse
and view below growing festivity
of thousands celebrating Jubilee.
The golden sun, concealed by thick, grey cloak,
an absentee amongst rejoicing folk,
who, holidaying, joyfully relax,
and laugh and chat and wave bright Union Jacks.
There, tiny children sway precariously
on shoulders, midst the human, heaving sea.
There, laughing teens and all-age family,
grandparents grey and aging OAP,
stand side by side to view this day's affair,
experiencing a day they closely share,
a Royal Pageant, gloriously seen
in recognition of our gracious Queen.
And rolling ever slowly, ageless by
Old Father Thames, 'neath dull, grey, leaden sky,
plays host to vessels, thousand strong, small, large,
accompanying the royal gold-red barge.
From bank and boat, there rises copious cheers
at sights unwitnessed for three hundred years.
June's England! Wet musicians sing and play,
soaked artists wetly capture such a day,
damp organisers bravely soldier through,
quite unperturbed by all they have to do.
None will forget this day, this glorious scene,
when thousands sang with joy, 'God Save Our Queen'.

MARGARET KEARLEY

A VERY SHORT POEM WITHIN
A SLIGHTLY LONGER POEM

She knows nothing at all about me
and I know nothing at all about her.
We have never met, you see.
Nevertheless, I felt inspired to compose
a haiku poem for her, as follows . . .

A Haiku For Her Majesty Queen Elizabeth II
On The Occasion Of Her Diamond Jubilee

Can you see me? Right
down here? Not on a coin. Not
on a stamp. Nowhere.

Perhaps, on a cold and rainy winter's day,
well after the Big Party is forgotten,
she may invite me over
and I can attempt to explain
the mystic meaning hidden deep within
the last word of the haiku.

Or we may just sit and watch the rainfall.
In silence.

WILLIAM WEAVINGS

GLORIANA

Elizabeth our Sovereign stood hours as heavens burst
Steadfastly saluting her fleet a thousand strong;
Dunkirk ships and man-powered, the royal row-barge first,
Then herald boats with chiming bells and song.

The public lined the river, soaked in the atmosphere,
On rooftops, crane tops, buildings, all the bridges filled;
Most were clutching brollies but thrilled with shouts and cheers,
Their flags a flap in the Pageant's winds.

The bright red firemen's launches sprayed out subversive jets,
Countering the Barrier's toil by topping up the Thames;
The gondolas and kayaks, the narrow boats five abreast,
Hooting in the gloom, doughty but drenched.

From Greenwich dawn to Chiswick, then back down past the Queen,
Through Tower Bridge up in salute and the Avenue of Sail,
Our craft chugged on till nightfall and didn't miss a beat,
Till we moored in the dark, drowned in the rain.

Was this the wettest party in three hundred and fifty years
Since Charles the Second's kingdom enjoyed a similar fest?
Ours drew inspiration from Canaletto's scene.
Pageantry's what Britain does best.

SUSAN BIGGIN

Hurrah! Queen Elizabeth II Reigns: A Ballad

Hurrah! Queen Elizabeth II reigns;
All glory to Jesus.
Sixty years on the throne she reigns;
All honour to Jesus.

By the grace of God,
Queen Elizabeth reigns!
For the love of God,
Queen Elizabeth reigns!
Proclaim to the world,
Queen Elizabeth reigns!
Her reign is peaceful;
Her reign is wonderful.

Born on April the twenty-first,
Nineteen twenty-seven,
She continues to achieve first,
Under the high Heaven.

In the year nineteen fifty-two,
She ascended the throne;
And promised to do her best too
On this her cherished throne.

As a young and leader valiant,
She set the tide to change;
Now old, but still very vibrant,
She's still bringing good change.

True to her pledge of great service,
To her dear Commonwealth,
With her vigour and great service,
She has brought common wealth.

Her life has been a great lesson;
In endurance and hope.
To all good leaders a lesson.
In belief like the Pope.

Her strength lies in her faithfulness
O'er the sixty years past.
Her success is in her gracefulness
That drives her to move fast.

The daughter of King George VI reigns;
Reigns after her father.
The daughter of Elizabeth reigns;
Made Queen as her mother.

Now look at two thousand and twelve;
And appreciate the feat.
Elizabeth is with number twelve;
Now in 10 Downing Street.

Her reign has brought tremendous growth
Over several decades.
Booming technological growth,
And countless major strides.

To world renowned leader we bow;
An enduring figure,
With good marks in the past and now,
A dynamic figure.

Duke Philip, the Queen's good husband,
We celebrate with you;
Sixty-five years as Queen's husband,
Sixty years on throne too.

BODE BABATUNDE

HER MAJESTY'S JUBILEE HOLIDAY

Through Admiralty Arch the guardsmen rode,
A passage of order, precision, beauty;
Red and gold signals of martial mode.
Little flags wave, remembering history.
Through the crowd a frisson, cheers, some clapping –
Here's Her Majesty to thank; a snapshot
As she passes quietly waving –
A reign for more than sixty years her lot.
Duties not sought after, nor evaded;
No personal benefit to accrue.
Devotion to Britannia never faded;
Her bond with her countrymen has come true.
Her public are there in reciprocation,
Their Queen to greet with love and admiration.

PAMELA DOUSE

Elizabeth, Our Queen

A diamond Queen, a glittering reign.
Devotion to duty, Great Britain's gain.
Crowds come to greet her from all round the world,
In London we cheer, Union flags are unfurled.
Twelve British Prime Ministers – that's a tough call,
With benign equanimity encountered them all.
Twelve US Presidents, met every one,
Elegance, dignity, duty is done.

Historic pageantry, royal tradition,
Each speech opening Parliament, a perfect rendition.
Ambassador, stateswoman, diplomat, leader,
In so many roles our countrymen need her.
A hand shaken in Ireland speeds conciliation,
Pressure of sovereignty, where's recreation?
A day at the races, Her Majesty's fun,
Ascot or Epsom, flat races are run.

Handing out honours, dubbing new knights,
Ermine and velvet, diamonds, bright lights.
The visits are endless, but with every good grace,
To relieve the monotony, let her have space
For family duties, no less demanding,
Young people requiring her wise understanding.
Mother and granny, great granny too,
Cuddlesome, selfless, loving and true.

A diamond Queen, a sparkling reign,
She's ruled through adversity, triumph and pain.
Suffering wars when so many died,
She wept for her people yet remained dignified.
With Philip beside her in sadness and splendour,
She strives and complies with a royal agenda.
Happy and glorious, gentle, serene,
Congratulations on your Diamond Jubilee,
Elizabeth, our Queen.

Rosa Johnson

OUR SERENE QUEEN

I understand from the press
That the Queen has a mobile phone
If she has, I wonder what is the ringing tone
National Anthem? Maybe not
In case left on when HM forgot

You can just imagine when in the State Coach
The horses would stop and Philip would reproach
But surmising all this does not detract
From her constant work which is quite a fact

In her 60 years as our loyal Queen
She is the greatest the world has ever seen
She does her job without any fuss
Long may she reign over us.

ALMA BRACE

JUBILATION?

A very British celebration
Of a German dynasty
Red, white and blue bunting
Made in a Chinese factory
Freezer full of party food
Produce of more than one EU country

Street party cancelled
For lack of an insurance policy
Trestle tables unused
Due to fears over health and safety
Extravagant celebrations
At a time of austerity

This may sound like
I view the occasion cynically
In truth
I support the monarchy
And applaud the Queen
On her Diamond Jubilee

ANDREW FISHER

ROYAL REFLECTIONS IN MOONLIGHT

It is late at night and here I'm alone
Seated on the terrace of my palace
Ruminating in the quiet moonlight.

As I stand on the threshold of the sixtieth
Anniversary of my reign as the
Monarch of Great Britain, multi-hued thoughts
Crowd my mind – memories of men who
Fashioned destiny, events that altered
History; reminiscences – some flood
My soul with exhilaration and joy;
Some with deep regrets at what might have been,
Sadness at what had been inevitable.

From the moment I heard, in a foreign
Land, of my father's passing away and
Consequently my succeeding to all
His responsibilities and duties
As Sovereign of the greatest empire ever
That was, till today to see my country
Face formidable challenges in the
Economic, financial as well as
The political spheres amidst global
Meltdown, it had been an arduous journey.
Looking back I wonder how I weathered
All the storms that blasted my country and
My own family.

That we have so far survived, enjoy a
Standard of life absent in many a
Nation previously affluent, is but
God's infinite grace, compassion towards our
Nation that had sent scores of missionaries
To Africa, China, India and several
Countries as martyrs to die, leave behind
Testimonies of sacrificial lives
Spent for His glory in the uplift of
Needy, poor, the sick and the unlettered.

In this strenuous journey I acknowledge
The unstinted support, encouragement
Of my husband whom God has given me.

As my people enjoy sound sleep feeling
Safe and hopeful for the morrow, I do

Pray to God to keep them, my family
And myself under the protection of
His wings and bless this country with a bright,
Secure, peaceful future.

Father, I commend my people and my
Country to your divine care, to keep them
Safe from all evil, grant all their needs and
Guide us all in paths You'll have us tread.

NITHIE VICTOR

CHESS

The aim of chess is to get the king,
to weave past pawns, rooks, knights and bishops
and then to his right, upright and pristine;
one must get past his queen.

Diamonds sparkling, twinkling, glittering,
blooming from the magma's depths, spluttering.
This cacophony of carbon.
Phoenix from the ashes perhaps.

Can you find celebration
amidst the fanfare of gunfire?
What sort of landmark date
is the coronation of revolution?
The gushing whirlpool of old regimes
starting to go down the sink.
Ousted monarchies, many there have been,
but not, (God save her), our Queen.

Beautiful is the first drop of water,
the crystal, diamond even, clear splish-splash
on parched, far journeyed lips.

Felicity is more so against its opposite.
It's always more check than checkmate.

PETER TSE

THE OUTFIT

Oh what a question, that's pressing me
What does one wear to one's jubilee?
I've heard Union Flag dresses
Are all the rage,
But one has never really
Caught that craze.
One could copy one's idol,
Go for the Gaga,
Though wearing a meat dress
Might make one look la-la.
One quite fancies, wearing a leotard,
Just like Madge – would it stretch that far?
Perhaps the best answer, is to ask Kate,
How hip is it these days, to co-ordinate.
But what about the corgis – what shall one do?
I think Union prints on my favourite two.

Now what about one's hair,
Never mind what to wear!
One could try out a beehive,
Just like Amy,
Though everyone has one -
Far too samey.
And what for a hat?
What colour, what shape?
I want for a design
To make everyone gape.
How about a telephone?
Already been done.
Perhaps giant confectionery,
One loves a cream bun.

Oh, but at last,
Now it's become clear,
I've known it all along,
What'll get the biggest cheer;
Plain Union Flag dress,
That's not enough,
But one that's
Diamond encrusted –
That's the stuff!

HANNAH DICKINSON

JUBILEE

Can't be bothered to put caps on for the title
That's how much it meant to me

Wish she would do a Bill Yates and give a lot away
Floating feat alas
And Elton in pinkl
Makes me think

If King George were here
He'd just slay a dragon
'N' put it on the table

Whoops!
Right name, wrong fable
Oh something like that
It's all from the same stable

Though in them days and knights of old
A monarch earned by tales told
Of foreign lands with bloody sword in hand

Anyway I blogged my wishes on Yahoo
And got eight thumbs up
So people do agree with my stuff
Though three red
Won't leave me stressing as I go to bed

Though with security so
Tight?
This thought, I'm sure, will wake me up in the middle of the night

. . . not

Why was the sex offender
Passed of as right?
Could this lead to Al-Qaeda
Sneaking it in
When the time was right?

Though with convicted thugs
In final picture calls
Just about
Says it all

STEPHEN PLANT

DIAMOND JUBILEE

It's good to see
The films of the Queen
She has done so much
She is our jewel
In the crown
She never frowns
Or says a bad word
She works hard
Like us all
On this great island

We love her so much
And who can say
A bad word
We've got to be
Positive
And enjoy the
Celebrations
It's once in a
Lifetime
And the memories
Will be kept
Like gold
Three cheers
For the
Diamond Jubilee

KENNETH MOOD

ELIZABETH OUR DIAMOND QUEEN

A charming little baby girl
Born many years ago
Had no idea what lay in store
As years would come and go

From carefree days of childhood
She grew and time passed by
She moved into a different world
And into the public eye

As daughter of our future king
A kindly man but, he
So sadly lost his life and so
Elizabeth then was Queen

With Philip ever by her side
The passing years have shown
How much she's loved both far and wide
As our love for her has grown

So, Elizabeth, for 60 years
We salute you as our Queen
And thank you for these many years
For you are our Diamond Queen

DORIS COWIE

JUBILEE POEM

Three cheers for the Queen on her special day
She's royal, true and steadfast in every single way
Three cheers for the Queen for carrying out her role
She always does her best and gives her heart and soul

Three cheers for the Queen, she has a unique style
For the people of Great Britain, she goes the extra mile
Three cheers for the Queen, she really is a star
Admirers – she has many, from both near and afar

Three cheers for the Queen, she never seeks the glory
I really do believe that she could tell us quite a story
Three cheers for the Queen, she's been monarch for sixty years
She's served her people well, through the laughter and the tears

Three cheers for the Queen, she's never let us down
There's no doubt about it, she's the *Diamond* in the crown
Three cheers for the Queen, she's really very cool
So here's a great big thank you from all at St Ed's School . . .

Three cheers for Her Majesty . . .
Hip, hip hooray, Hip, hip hooray, Hip, hip hooray

ELLA ROSE QUIGLEY

QUEEN OF HEARTS

This quite remarkable lady
Our monarch, she can do no wrong
Loyal servant to her subjects
For sixty years and still going strong

With a deep sense of civic duty
She maintains her ceremonial role
Tirelessly she works all year
The coronation oath is her goal

She is our Ma'am, our Majesty
The figurehead of this nation
Defender of the faith
Our muse, our inspiration

Yet she cannot go on forever
There will be abdication one of these days
But she will always remain special
Our Queen of hearts always

BOB HARRIS

JUBILEE 2012

Find me at the place where the city runs out
Where the roads meet
That open bit of space between the corner of the park and the end of your street

I can see the children play,
Two bountiful dogs lose and find their tails
Oblivious of the drifting and circling crowds around them –
The gathering throngs,
This little pocket of the city throbs with the life of the street
BBQ smells and the pub band's rock songs

I can see an elderly man in the intermittent sun on a garden seat,
He chases a home-grown pea on a tri-colour paper plate
And wistfully watches the future growing up, setting in
London is on the roll-down screen, the palace shines bright
Like a hymn
And a jubilant banner frees itself of the centre table and flaps about his feet

A couple tentatively hold each other, second date and cringing with youth
In the heart of this clumsy, eclectic street
The man with the ripped shorts and the grandmother in the waterproof
And the teenagers clashing in colours and overdoing everything,
Twist and fling to the tune of the bands,
Whilst chocolate buttons from red, white and blue cupcakes melt in small, sticky hands

I listened as the choir sang,
As the clouds lurked and loomed,
Offering us fleeting glimpses
Of that old friend
The sun
And caught by all corners of this place
I smiled – I could be anyone

I am moved by fancies
That are curled around these images and cling,
I have seen what we can be, when together, when free
A view from God,
What a bright, fleeting, delicate thing

Find me at the close of day,
At the place where the roads converge and meet,
Alone, but now I can see the street, the subtleties I usually miss
And I connect this city, our magnificent nation,
I am one of millions of grinning, tapping feet
That could tread any way from this.

ZOE GRIFFITHS

22

DIAMONDS FOR THEM

The Queen will give them food
She will hand to them aid
They will begin to crave
For a much better life

The Queen will give them diamonds
They will start their enterprise
They will not suffer hungry
Their eyes will open – they'll see

The Queen will hold their hands
And lead them to the stars
Their galaxies will glow
They will want to learn more

MUHAMMAD KHURRAM SALIM

THE QUEEN IN MAJESTY

It all turned out lovely
From Derby Day to the balcony,
The four days of celebrations
For the Queen's Diamond Jubilee.

A reign of 60 years is plenty
In times as these for sure,
But our Queen surprised many
When she opened up her doors.

If the Derby was lovely at Epsom
The Flotilla along the River Thames,
Was as never before, but for Cleopatra
And for us she rode the waves by.

To end the multi-talented pop concert
A kiss on the hand from Prince Charles,
Who had seen so many beautiful wonders
But this was a wonderful charm.

And the people to throng the streets
On every occasion there to meet,
A glance at Her Majesty as she passed by
Oh what a lovely birthday treat!

TREVOR POOLE

HER MAJESTY . . .

Elizabeth, a sweet young lady,
With a lovely smiling face,
But soon she would lose her father
And a world she would have to face,
Then, on those tiny shoulders
A nation she would lead,
Grieving for her father,
Her heart within did bleed,
With courage she wore the mantle,
The new monarch she became,
The role heavy on her shoulders,
To fulfil was her aim,
She, as a Christian lady
Turned to God to guide her way,
And through her 60 years of 'leading'
He has been her strength and stay,
She has led by example,
Through days of joy and days of tears,
Gracious in her dealings,
With Earth's peoples through the years,
She has travelled through many continents
And sailed o'er oceans wide,
Accompanied by her husband,
She has borne calm and stormy tide,
By grace she has led out nation,
Steadfast in her role,
The monarchy resting on her shoulders,
Within her firm control,
Sixty years ago she was given
The mantle of a queen,
And still she continues to lead us,
In that role supreme,
She is a woman well respected,
She has dined in great halls,
She has strolled with Earth's Presidents
And conversed with great and small,
She has lived her life in 'service',
To the peoples of many lands,
Britain and the Commonwealth,
Safe within her hands,
She has shown love for God's creatures
And respect for all Mankind,

She has fulfilled her role impeccably
And all she was assigned,
Daily she graciously serves us
And diligent will remain,
Showing her Christian principles,
Throughout her long, demanding reign,
The world it has watched her,
With her dignity and grace
And celebrates her 60 years
In the role she has embraced,
She is a lovely human being,
An example to us all,
A humble, Christian woman,
Who, as our Queen, has stood tall . . .

JUNE HARDMAN

OH! FIGUREHEAD

Oh! Figurehead! Oh! Figurehead!
Let your crown sparkle tho' heavy as lead
To the gummed profile hold fast and be wed
You keep your palaces, we'll keep our heads!
Oh! Figurehead! Oh! Figurehead!
Let the photographers rot in their beds
Dismiss sweaty gossip of romps at Hickstead
(Make Sunday Tabloids retract 'til they're bled)
Oh! Figurehead! Oh! Figurehead!
Ermine and squirming in corridors red
Your treasures and trials are openly said
The gold-leaf is flaking, spoiled and shed.
Oh! Figurehead! Oh! Figurehead!
So hounded and rounded and mocked when you're dead
Your sceptre and garter lay disconnected
We'll eat the cake – while you earn the bread . . .
Oh! Figurehead!

BARLEY ROBINSON

THE QUEEN

The Queen, the Queen, you are a star
For you have reigned for 60 years so far.

Four wonderful children you have got
And your grandchildren are a special lot!

Buckingham Palace is where you live
To charities world-wide a lot you give.

Your corgis are your special pets
Will you ever take them to the vets?

Royal visits are a must
You're the one we all trust.

Would you like some tea and cake?
What a feast that will make.

Come and celebrate the Jubilee
With all your friends and family!

HARVEY COTTON

DIAMOND JUBILEE – YEAR 2012

Sixty years ago Queen Elizabeth II started her reign on the throne, in 1952.
It had been a milestone for Her Majesty serving the United Kingdom.
Also the Queen marked her Diamond Jubilee as a 'humbling experience'
It brought many families and friends in the neighbourhood celebrating together.
The celebrations of Diamond Jubilee were shared both in the UK
And the Commonwealth countries.
The Queen has been an excellent sovereign, also seeing changes for 60 years.
She has kept in a very calm manner during difficult times.
Saw the experiences of Silver and Golden Jubilees.
Thank you Your Majesty, for being there by serving the United Kingdom for 60 years.
Congratulations on your Diamond Jubilee year.

ERROL BAPTISTE

THE QUEEN'S DIAMOND JUBILEE

I'm the Queen, I'm the Queen, I'm the Queen,
For sixty years the Queen I've been,
Since nineteen-fifty-two, the Queen's been me,
This year is my Diamond Jubilee.

Look Philip, it's all about me,
The street parties,
The cheering, smiling crowds,
Oh look Philip, I'm on TV.

I've practised my waving
And fixed on my smile,
By train, plane and car we'll travel this land,
To celebrate my reign.

Put on comfy shoes,
I'll be on my feet for hours,
Gather the ladies,
To collect all the flowers.

The crowds they are thronging,
My people, what joyful sounds they make,
I've walked and waved
Till feet, hands and face ache.

Sixty years I've sat on the throne,
I've served my people and country without a moan,
This day is all about me,
So why has no one made me
A nice cup of tea?

CINDY FAULKNER

HM Queen Elizabeth II

Her shoulders straight, her head held high
a smile on her face and yet there's a silent sigh,
walking through the crowds, shaking a hand,
majestically calm, she's the Queen of our land.

Her regal beauty captures hearts everywhere
wherever she goes, people long to be there
to see her pass by and catch one of her smiles
so they can cheer for her they walk for miles.

Her life is not as easy as it first appears to be
the duties followed by the Queen's responsibility
she carries on regardless with her royal task
drawing strength from experiences of her past.

For so many years now she's worn the crown
there were often days which made her frown
having to take care with every step along the way
wishing that tomorrow may be an ordinary day.

Monica Partridge

Queen Elizabeth

Elizabeth is a grand old dame
It's all in the magnificent name!

Lizziebeth, Libby, Beth and Liz,
All these variations are a real whizz!

She works really hard to keep our country great
We'll stay top of the world at this rate!

She loves her corgis, loves her dogs
Even though they smell like hogs.

'God save our Queen,' I hear you shout
Of this fact there is no doubt.

A greater monarch there had never been,
All the other countries are jealously green!

Niamh Gollan (10)

QUEENIE, QUEENIE

Queenie, Queenie, look at me,
I'm celebrating your Jubilee,
I'm waving flags in front of your eyes,
Having a feast and eating chocolate pies.

I'm partying all day and all night,
With my friends, oh what a sight!
We cheer, we shout, we wave, we cry,
We hope the sun comes to keep us dry.

'God save the Queen,' you hear us cheer,
In our hearts you're always near,
The Royal Anthem blasts out loud,
On this day we are so proud!

God Save Our Queen!

KIANA GOLLAN (9)

JUBILEE, JUBILATE

On a cold, wet Sunday
Day of the Jubilee,
I chose to stay at home, keep dry,
Watch the River Pageant on TV.

I know that down our road they had
A celebration tea,
I saw it signed and thought it good,
That it was all for free.

The day care centre on our street,
Venue for the big event,
But although it wasn't far away,
I'm still glad I never went.

But passing by in sunshine,
Bunting still across the gate,
The invitation notice there,
Though by now, some weeks too late.

I came around to thinking,
A tea party could be fun,
If the weather had been kinder
And the day was blessed with sun.

JOYCE WALKER

MARGARET ELISABETH

Years stood it's place on sideboard corner
Two sisters smile in frozen monochrome,
'Tis one still reigns, beloved Monarch
As the other rests 'neath marbled stone.
There lived these names my own dear mother,
For loved year of birth blessed April's green.
Count many year's coy spring's arrival,
Born very year of well loved Queen.
In well-live life 'twas ever regal
Stands sad room festooned of royalty,
Each marriage, birth 'tis born in china
How would have loved Queen's Jubilee,
Proud stand of dust beloved collection
Though since mourned passing never grown,
Still smiling royal stand ceramic,
Glazed eyes there stare, cold room, alone.

'Tis foot-trod gravel marks my walking
As graveyard primrose mourns spring's fade,
With deep respect, 'twould be her bidding
On marble plaque, small flag is laid.

JOHN CATES

JUBILEE

Dignity born of duty
That began its flowering
Sixty years ago,
Style that has grown over time,
A style that has embraced compassion
Blended with wisdom,
Smiles and colours.
Love for family and humankind
Continue to shine through.
Jubilee.

DENISE KNIGHT

THANK YOU HER MAJESTY, FROM NABURN VILLAGE

Thank you, Her Majesty,
for awakening this sleepy Yorkshire village by the Ouse,
typically serene
but now on the edge of anticipation.

British flags fly free and proud
as the community rally
for once, in unison
honouring your Grand Day.

The front street is set for the party,
a royal reason
to dance and laugh
amidst such dark, brooding times.

The old reminisce, the young stir with possibilities . . .
there is something for everyone
as modernity and tradition, the ancient and new,
merge and mingle in rhythmic fusion.

As evening descends,
the silver moon rises in quiet witness upon the darkening sky
and lights glitter and twinkle
like infinite scattered diamonds
across the sparkling waters of the Ouse.

Music reverberates, laughter rings in the air.
This Yorkshire village awakes from slumber,
with hope not forgotten, with pride still intact . . .
Thank you, Her Majesty . . .

JACQUELINE ZACHARIAS

THE QUEEN

Sixty years on
Where has all that time gone?
Her Majesty's devotion to duty
Steadfastly goes on and on.

She appears to effortlessly
Take everything in her stride,
Such a perfect lady in every way,
Loyally performing her duties,
In such a dignified way.

She's a dedicated ambassador
For our country indeed,
She'll be a difficult act to follow,
A true legend, destined to lead.

JOAN CATHERINE IGESUND

HRH QUEEN ELIZABETH II

You looked radiant on your special day
I'd like to put my arms around you just to say,
You are the best thing in this country.
You've had your ups, you've had your downs,
But you never seem to frown.
Your family shower you with love,
Even those in Heaven above.
Yourself and the Duke waved as you passed by in car,
(Chesterfield 1977),
You radiate happiness wherever you are.
Hope your days are filled with love and fun
And your reign goes on and on.
Your reign will last many years more . . .
And will be loved forever I am sure.

E RIGGOTT

THE DIAMOND JUBILEE

Children of today will tell their children that they were there that day.
Over 1,000 ships and boats of all shapes and sizes moved along
the Thames that day to celebrate the Queen's Diamond Jubilee.
Over one million spectators lined the embankments on either side
of Europe's noblest river to revel in the occasion.
Throughout the pageant, music could be heard wafting up from the boats:
popular sea shanties, nautical airs, pipes, horns, bells,
Handel's glorious Water Music . . .
On its steady journey to Tower Bridge the armada passed many wonderful
iconic, London landmarks, including the Palace of Westminster, the London Eye
and Waterloo Bridge, where Wordsworth composed his immortal ode,
'Upon Westminster Bridge'.
As the flotilla moved from one section to another, from bridge to bridge,
newly painted Canalettos unfolded before your very eyes.
And when the Queen passed the spectators on her Royal Barge,
the magnificent Spirit of Chartwell, its ornate golden prow moving majestically
through the water, they morphed into tumultuous seas of cheering, singing,
flag waving, happy, loving, congenial humanity.
It was beautiful!
And what a finale!
Not only were there more moving salutes to the Queen –
by Tower Bridge, the HMS Belfast veterans and the Beefeaters, but also,
perhaps one of the highlights of the show, a group of young singers
from the Royal College of Music,
drenched and bedraggled by the appalling rain.
in true British spirit, singing their patriotic hearts out to
'Land of Hope and Glory', 'Rule Britannia' and
'God Save the Queen'.
They were magnificent.
The whole day was magnificent.
It was living history. A once in a life-time experience.
The pomp and pageantry were of epic proportions that only the British can do.
Nothing had been seen like it for 350 years, since the reign of Charles II.
Britain was the envy of the world that day.
'Dull would he be of soul who could pass by
A sight so touching in its majesty . . .'

SYDNEY WRAGG

THE QUEEN, SHE IS A DIAMOND

Many a certain age, remember the day
bunting decorated street parties
Souvenir mug, coin were given, ate cheese in bread,
jelly with Smarties
Time to recognise, 'she is a diamond'
at this her 60 year reign as Queen
A Jubilee festival, celebrations and events,
organised to follow, to be seen
Elizabeth II, a figurehead much loved,
respected, at the heart of the nation
Citizens to join with activities,
praising Your Majesty's status and station

As an ordinary person, subject of the realm,
I admire you from afar
Would I think be nervous in your company,
would love to drive your car
Your smile lights up, meeting strangers,
touching an outstretched hand
Making time as you do, with children waiting
to give flowers, to stand
Evident your enjoyment of horses, owning,
racing one deserves a shout
Love for the country life, seen,
when dressed in wellies out and about
People seek your presence here in this country and abroad
Your popularity, recognition of the role you undertake has soared
Confident, being at ease with,
in the company of a different varied sort
Foreign heads of state, film stars,
soldiers for their bravery, they fought
You enter a room where all eyes are upon you,
with pleasure you are seen
When backstage, a gathered, waiting cast wait, excited, enthusiastic, keen

An eventful family life during your reign had followed over the years
A great grandmother again, Isla, thirteenth in line,
happiness with tears
With Prince Philip together in good company,
a strength in marriage
Seen by the outside world together,
waving, along in a fairytale carriage
Your many duties require varied adjustment, control and skill

Wonder at wearing of the crown,
at horse guards high on a horse and still

Journey on Thames water planned,
a flotilla passing the royal barge
The Gloriana, leading a pageant,
a festival of boats, little and large
Flying their colours, 1,000 boats at any one spot,
90 minutes to pass
Saluting the Queen, Wandsworth to Tower Bridge,
a spectacle, sheer class
Featuring the next day, a festival,
a Buckingham Palace concert musical
Guest singers, spectators, after the rain,
Join Tom Jones, 'It's Not Unusual'

May you, as Queen,
enjoy with us the Jubilee events uniting the people
Reflect on the esteem for you, when passing under St Paul's steeple
Long may you continue, the People's Queen,
a walkabout in the street
In recognition of 60 years on the throne, a bank holiday, a bonus, a treat
A woman of stature, a focus of stability in a dynamic, evolving state
Figurehead for the nation, the Royal Family,
Queen Elizabeth the Great

RON CONSTANT

JUBILATION

Put up the bunting, search out the flags
Place the flasks and sandwiches in your bags
Then we're off to London on trains and coaches
Getting so excited as the time approaches.
Alight at Westminster, go down to the river
Feel the excitement, you're all of a quiver
Our Queen's Diamond Jubilee starts off today
Let's get ready to cheer her 'Hip, hip hooray!'
She is the best there is, our lovely Liz
Works hard all year round, she does the biz
For sixty long years she has now reigned
Not ever, not once has she complained.
With good old Prince Philip by her side
They travel around our countryside
Elegant as always, she is small and neat
Chatting to those who have come to greet.
She came down the Thames on a barge
Covered in flowers and very large
Crowds of people waving and singing
Bells on the first boat constantly ringing.
All the people cheering and shouting
Pleased they had come on this Sunday outing
Children tired, people soaked with rain
Yes, they would do it all over again.
It is a day they will never forget
And all of the people they had met
They could tell you everywhere they had been
Up to London to look at our Queen.

DOROTHY FULLER

ERII

Buckingham Palace, royal, regal eyrie
Home from home when tired and weary
To chill out from one's queenly kingdom
From trying, tiresome, humdrum officialdom
Stroke the corgis, wagging and happy
Sometimes, like Philip, somewhat snappy
Now and again they get on one's wick
Give them a biccy, does the trick
Don one's old slippers, this time's for me
Put one's feet up, sip a large G and T
Maid's now waiting for bath to fill
Can't wait to dive in for a swill
Royal duties can get one down
I still have nightmares of Gordon Brown
Even the Lords are somewhat fuddy-duddy
Some of their pasts decidedly muddy
It won't be long before dinner gong
I hope nothing in the kitchen goes wrong
Tonight it's traditional toady in the hole
Followed by my favourite pud, Regal Role
After dinner, Corrie and Jeremy Kyle
I like watching morons once in a while
As you know, one is rather well read
Tonight it's Cath Cookson and so to bed
Preparing for a jolly good night's sleep
Not very exciting, but beats counting sheep
One's riding tomorrow over Windsor's stiles
Side-saddle of course, with old Farmer Giles

IAN TOMLINSON

ELISHEVA; PROTECTOR OF MAN . . .

At Silver we smile
To Golden we applaud
And Diamond?
We celebrate until fifth and full.
Watching your crown
Transcend to this new concoction.
As it grew brighter and stronger,
You crinkled and slowed,
No longer the speed of spots,
But still the breath of death.
We show love and honour,
Though some don't feel.
You address the nation,
To reduce our fears.
So sit high in your loyal position,
Which flew down upon no one's wishes.
Your age exceeds the early sexagenarian throne,
Though it was crafted before your conception.
So smile and wave,
These are your flags and Great Seal,
Just know . . . we lie, we steal for your paper feel.
Enjoy your days, for
It is now the sixth and
Not yet have you become a myth.

SARAH JANE BURROWS

A MOVING MOMENT

From that day it rained, nothing laid still
You were just a young, beautiful woman
When you became Queen

The country was still on ration
And everything was still in fashion

And you weren't alone
The nation bound together

As you sat on your throne
You were anointed and swore your oath
With spoken words

The flags flew proudly
Bright colours blew on a windy day
They all camped out on the wet sidewalk way

The band played their music
They danced on the street
And were a cheerful crowd

As they marched up and down the street
The horses well groomed
The fireworks lit up the skyline

She uplifted their mood
And as she drew strength
From waving to the crowd

Through this splendid day
On this timeless past

KATIE TURNEY

A FAN

Staring at the colours
Dancing before me,
Wow!
The parades, the music, the people,
All here for her.
Flying flags, flapping in the wind in every direction.
Noise. A lot of noise.
Cheering, singing,
Excited children standing on their father's shoulders,
Just to get a glimpse of her.
Crowds fighting to the front –
Pushing, shoving.
'There she is!'
I glance up
And there she is, waving at me from her shiny car,
Zooming by.

And there I am waving back.
'God Save the Queen,' they scream.
God Save our Queen.

REBECCA O'DONOVAN

DIAMOND JUBILEE

The iron clang of bells, the thunder of cannon
Honour her name, to whom people love to hail.

Beacons burn, lasers light the realm up.
Elizabeth, sixty years a queen. The nation

Placed the burden of the crown on her head.
Since then time has flown. The head that bears

The diadem has grown grey. Today the faithful
Gather. Let us hear vavuzelas, pipes

And drums. Salute the icon of the Empire.
Sixty years of reign with peace and honour.

M ATHAR ATHERTON

DIAMOND JUBILEE

Diamond Jubilee
What does it mean to me?
Sixty years she has been
Our glorious Queen
A Diamond Jubilee

Stoical and dutiful, yet young at heart
By protocol and ceremony kept apart
Yet as much a part of life as a cup of tea

Enduring symbol, our nation's Queen
Great Britain personified, all that it means
Proud and patriotic we should be

Such an achievement – sixty years
Through war and peace, joy and tears
Through times of want and prosperity

Keeping her counsel, with waves and smiles
Serving the people of this green and pleasant isle
Reminding us of how we ought to be

Not sentimental but inspiring in all
A sense of service and standing tall
Believing in the best for our community

We celebrate not just a number of days
But a woman of faith in all her ways
Finding her strength in His divinity

So I pray for our gracious, noble Queen
That through all that lies in years unseen
Our God her guide and strength will be

Diamond Jubilee
That's what it means to me
In all my life I've known
One monarch on the throne
May she continue Deo volente.

SARAH GLEAVE

THE DIAMOND JUBILEE

As a daughter she provided happiness,
As a mother she became a figurehead,
As a grandmother she had wisdom,
As a great grandmother she has become an inspiration.

She was a young girl
With a royal soul,
Born to reign,
And protect her country.

As a daughter she provided happiness,
As a mother she became a figurehead,
As a grandmother she had wisdom,
As a great grandmother she has become an inspiration.

She was a mother,
Loyal and wise,
Her journey to protecting her kingdom,
Was well on its way.

As a daughter she provided happiness,
As a mother she became a figurehead,
As a grandmother she had wisdom,
As a great grandmother she has become an inspiration.

She was a grandmother,
Head of the Commonwealth,
With the Union Jack
She sailed the sea.

As a daughter she provided happiness,
As a mother she became a figurehead,
As a grandmother she had wisdom,
As a great grandmother she has become an inspiration.

She was a great grandmother,
Proud and pretty,
Her journey to protecting the kingdom
Is sixty years on.

As a daughter she provided happiness,
As a mother she became a figurehead,
As a grandmother she had wisdom,
As a great grandmother she has become an inspiration.

Jubilee! Jubilee!
That's all you're going to hear,
From London to Canada,
Which is many miles from here.

As a daughter she provided happiness,
As a mother she became a figurehead,
As a grandmother she had wisdom,
As a great grandmother she has become an inspiration.

JEMMA YOUNGMAN

HONEY

The noise -
the lowly hum,
rising to a right Royal pitch.

The buzz -
the lowly drone,
anger gathering at your throne.

And you -
with lonely flights,
to far and wide,
leading on this swarming throng
to Headier heights:
to rest.

Be still.

Where, O where
is thy sting?

ALISON COOKE

What A Diamond

Great Britain and the Commonwealth
For 60 years she has led
Such an historical achievement
From a monarch and famous figurehead

On news of her father's death
In '52 she ascended the throne
Cutting short her trip to Treetops
From Kenya she returned home

Princess Elizabeth Alexandra Mary
Was born eighty-six years ago
Not knowing what her future held
It was already planned that was so

Having been educated at home
In French, history, maths and art
It was from the age of eleven
With the Girl Guides she became a part

She met her future husband in 1934
Philip Mountbatten was his name
He was in the Royal Navy
His life would never be the same

Wearing a Norman Hartnell dress
She wed her beau in '47
With eight bridesmaids and two pages
A complete match made in heaven

From 1948 on they were to have four kids
Charles, Anne, Andrew and Edward
A new future as busy parents
Many happy years to look forward

Their family has now expanded
With grandchildren galore
Keeping them up with modern times
And new ventures to explore

The Queen had made over 200 visits
To countries spanning the world
Mostly Australia, Canada, New Zealand
And a few remote islands to behold

She has launched twenty-three ships
Met five astronauts that have been in space
There aren't many people
Who can forget this royal face

She still loves her corgis
Not forgetting the horses too
Keeping her hand in at the stables
Telling the grooms what to do

So in her 60 years as sovereign
What will the future bring?
More monumental times? Who knows
For Elizabeth R, our Queen!

DAWN WILLIAMS-SANDERSON

SIXTY GLORIOUS YEARS

We had a television, one of the very few
Friends asked to visit, the Coronation to view
The day was dismal with rain clouds about
Yet thousands braved the weather to cheer and shout
Our view was a small picture in black and white
All in our crowded room looked on with delight
To see our lovely princess crowned as our Queen
That day was captured in people's hearts as in a dream
Now sixty years have passed as we look back on your reign
You have seen this country through pleasures and pain
The nation loves you and we are bursting with pride
With your walkabout with Prince Philip by your side
Your private and personal life has not been easy we know
Children tug your heartstrings but they finally grow
We see you like ourselves, as a mother and nan
Whilst you reign as our Queen, united we stand
Your radiant smile had cheered us through peace and war
United we pray you will reign over us for ever more

LEONARD A G BUTLER

THE QUEEN'S DIAMOND JUBILEE

A sense of excitement fills the air,
The crowds are dense, no room to spare.
People have travelled across land and sea,
To celebrate the Queen's Jubilee.

The mood is electric as tensions all soar
And suddenly cheering erupts with a roar,
As a boat with bells chiming heralds the start
Of a sight so glorious it gladdens the heart.

Gloriana, royally decked, magnificent to see,
The rowers dipping every blade in perfect harmony.
She led a thousand vessels and flags of all the nations,
This vast armada sharing in the joyful celebrations.

The royal barge, a glittering sight,
Aboard was the Queen in shining white.
Millions cheered, the sound uproarious,
The day was truly happy and glorious.

Then the concert, a dazzling affair,
Even the Coldstream Guards were there.
Famous stars sang on the stage,
Delighting an audience of every age.

Cunningly lit the palace displayed
Scenes and colours in brilliant cascade.
Resplendent in gold, the Queen smiled in delight
As a million fireworks illumined the night.

On the final day of the Jubilee,
Led by the Household Cavalry,
In open landau the Queen rode in style,
Enchanting all people with a wave and a smile.

Marching bands played with skill and panache,
The drums loud beat, the cymbals clash.
The crowds went wild at this grand display,
Cheering, 'God Save The Queen, Hip hip Hooray!'

And as the procession passed out of view,
Outside the palace the multitude grew.
The happy Queen waved to all she could see,
Celebrating the Diamond Jubilee.

The Red Arrows and the Memorial Flight
Flew overhead to screams of delight.
For the Queen it has been a time of bliss,
Her very own Annus Mirabilis.

PHYLLIS CHOPPEN

A NATION SPARKLES

The red, white and blue
Streamers are high
The sky a bit grey
Won't dampen the day
Hip hip hooray
We're here for the Queen
Three cheers today
Diamond Jubilee
Long may she reign
Eminent and revered.
The red, white and blue
Banners and flags
We're having a blast
This spectacular day.
Don't care about the
Weather, under umbrellas
We'll watch the flotilla
And cheer the parade
We'll dance in the street
Dressed up real neat
We'll cheer as we're proud
A partying crowd.
Hip hip hooray
We're here for the Queen
Regally serene
Diamond Jubilee
This is our day
And the nation is proud.

PETER PAYNE

Queen Elizabeth II

I am Elizabeth Alexandra Mary, the Queen,
With sapphire eyes and lily-white skin,
And hair of deepest oak in chocolate curls,
In lucent satin gown with pastel swirls,
Of Tudor pink rose; palest leeks of green
And shamrock, purple thistle, maple leaf,
Protea, sunburst wattle, wheat of gold
And lotus flower, fern, mother of pearl.
With diadem kissed by diamond droplet gleams
And golden shoes peeping with garnet studded heels.

I am Rebecca Mary Joyce, eleven years of age,
With emerald eyes and skin of honey beige,
In frock of white broiderie anglaise twirls
And knitted pink cardigan; buttons pearl,
A shamrock brooch clasped to purple gabardine,
In crowd bespeckled with pearly kings and queens.
Water drenched, waving handkerchiefs and hats,
At Queen Elizabeth, rock of our land,
In crown of St Edward, iced droplets teem
And my poppy shoes pinken as we glisten in the rain.

Julie Elaine Lancaster neé Durn

CONGRATULATIONS MA'AM 2012

The journey you have made we hold in high esteem,
Loyalty never overshadowed, always generating a warm beam,
Your smile always highlights any obvious situation,
Instantly causing one to recognise genuine consideration.

Travelling has always been part of a yearly programme,
Strengthening the bond between our country's culture ma'am,
Showing interest in developing ideas, encouraging progress,
Emulating a warm peace, instilling confidence for future success.

Support from your family carries so much loyalty,
One can feel the presence of loving stability,
Sharing your success, involving their lives,
Shows volumes of admiration and respect as each member strives.

Foundation from a family comes from a mother,
Who gives advice when necessary to one or other,
Guiding their pathway to unwind with grace,
A formula which blossoms and develops at a steady pace.

Sixty years is a very long time,
Pages have been turned, history has been redesigned,
History, which governs our lives, in just moments of time,
Strengthening each day, in faith, trust and love – obvious signs.

We are all looking forward to celebrating your sixty year reign,
A time the nation will remember with joy, again and again.
When the nation plays loving homage to our beloved Queen,
Thanking and honouring her name and what it means.

LORNA TIPPETT

THE QUEEN'S DIAMOND JUBILEE

It was a fantastic party,
A 1953 street party I was told,
The bunting and flags were flying,
So authentic, colourful, so bold.

The atmosphere was electric,
The scene was thoroughly set,
The old piano was belting out,
Old favourites we won't forget.

The sandwiches were tasty, egg, ham,
Salmon, even potted meat,
Crisps and fancy cakes galore,
A sing a long with tapping of feet.

The cake was rather splendid
And champagne for everyone,
I have never enjoyed a party
As much as I did that special one.

So thanks to Yorkshire Country Women,
For all the planning of the hall,
It was much appreciated,
Thank you from one and all.

MARY PARKER

JU-BEE-LATION

Yes, I was around in fifty-three,
The Coronation there to see,
Television had not long been born,
But we had one on that lovely morn.
Unfortunately tho' not in colour,
Everything else in the day was much duller,
We've followed her reign throughout the years,
Happiness, sadness, toils and tears!
We watched her children born and grow,
Dear Charles and Anne, they love her so.
Now all have families of their own,
And still she sits upon our throne.
She never shies away from duties,
Always there and perfectly suited,
For years her mum was by her side,
Always happy, so much pride!
Still with her partner, bold, upright,
The Duke of Edinburgh is still so bright.
Now sixty years have been and gone
And as strong as ever she still reigns on.
All eyes were on that celebratory week,
The wonder, the colour, the pomp so sleek!
Then trooping the colour, what more can one say?
A wonderful end! Shout hip hip hooray!

JOHN BRIGHT

THE ROYAL THREAD
(A SONNET FOR THE 2012 JUBILEE)

Illustrious line of royalty is like
A golden thread with jewelled beads along;
Some bright, some shining, others dark or dull,
Each lends it colour to its nation's life.
Sometimes a bead is broken or pulled off.
The thread remains unbroken, even so;
Lies quietly waiting for the time to come
For restoration by the rightful jewel.
The jewels are chosen for us. Nature rules.
Choice is not ours, we must submit to that.
Some demand choice. Results are argument,
Strife, ridicule and discontinuance.
Let's learn acceptance and together say,
'Praise present Diamond on Diamond Day.'

PAMELA TURNER

REIGN OF DIAMONDS

D iamond lustrous
I llustrious in our land
A dmired Queen and
M onarch of our time
O bservant, ever serving
N ever veering
D iamond Majesty

J ubilant Jubilee
U plifting hearts and
B rightening all our land
I n joyous celebration
L ingering the treasured years
E voking the gaiety and tears
E nkindling recollection.

LORNA TROOP

NOWHERE TO HIDE

The society that refuses to change
Outworn ideas outweigh progress
Who vaunts doing down millions
Knowing millions will not bite back

Young Socialists uphold tradition
When their time in government comes
Young Socialists once they were
Now they are lords of the realm

I would be ashamed to turn coat
No these old hats are widely admired
You add to the letters after your name
The longer the list the better

Out in the streets it is downhill
A million young men and women
Lie in bed with no occupation
To please the fat the tribe in tow

You are clever to get on board
Prosper those who shout their legion
I am ashamed to be British
To live among the supporters of royalty

I will die out on a limb
In no-man's-land a child of my time
Listening to you trimmers, counterfeiters
Scum of the earth thumbing at us all

SIMON WARREN

THE QUEEN'S JUBILEE

The 3rd of June
The rain came down
Jubilee celebrations
In honour of the crown

We celebrated in the rain
The Queen's Jubilee
Her sixty year reign
Of the country

The whole nation united
Young and old, fat and thin, happy and sad, black and white
And not too far away
The Queen could be sighted
On a rainy day
That actually turned out alright

Crowds lined the banks of the Thames
Waving their drenched and soggy flags
Thousands of boats travelled across the Thames
As the crowd cheered and screamed, waving their flags

Flags could be seen all over the place
On almost every building
Some had the Union Jack printed on their face
And the National Anthem, some decided to sing

Laughter and happiness could be heard despite the wet
Not a face in the crowd could be seen that was glum
On a memorable day
And a day that was full of laughter and fun

Like a mother, she has a lot of love to share
Stands proud amongst her family
And to those who fight for the country
She gives so much care
As she stands amongst her family.

HANNAH NICHOLLS

MY QUEEN

All my life Her Majesty has been my loyal Queen
Proud I am of our heritage and what she has been
Coronation day set sadly years before my time
But my mother was there; spoke of your face divine
My devoted Queen, never stepping a foot out of place
Always elegant, refined, composed and full of grace
From a princess to a queen, quite unexpectedly too soon
Responsibility that you hold, dedication through and through
Imagine that fear you felt on that glorious, splendid day
In your youth the sense of duty was ever to prevail
Your sadness, loss of a dear father, faced it all alone
The heart heavy, a crown, placed on the royal throne
Sure there is always a smile from that dainty physique
Oh my Queen, a mould so perfect, so gentle, so unique
I know you suffered from trials, difficulties in times past
Death, disaster had wavered, but you held on steadfast
Stood strong, a pillar of strength, your history remains today
I wonder if ghosts of past generations would return to say
Your attire, so carefully planned, always so appropriate, so grand.
Always the petite brooch pin, welcome greeting with hand
So much altered over age of time, you have experienced it all
Sixty years served with right or wrong, never to stumble or fall
Centuries of ancestors, books written, all have been read
My Queen, your country is grateful, people speak, enough said
The golden wedding came, an invitation sent to the door
A royal garden party, my parents were chosen to go
Weeks of excitement, a special tea in a diplomatic tent
You spoke to my mother, if only you knew what that meant
Delicate china, dainty cakes, presented a replica of you
The band played, sun shone on this magnificent venue
My Queen, your knowledge vast, this strange world around
Aware of your people, their bitter cries and silent sounds
Those daily duties without fail, even when the body slows
My Queen, I salute you, vitality and spirit continues to grow
Kings have ruled leaving trails of antiquities for us to relate
But my Queen, your long reign we will never again create
The Jubilee celebrations well deserved, right to commemorate.

A true, faithful, exceptional, dutiful, noble head of state
So my queen, these simple words are written from the heart
Forever your loyal subject, I am privileged to have played a part.

ANNE WILLIAMS

THE DIAMOND QUEEN

In nineteen fifty-two, one February day
King George the Sixth passed peacefully away.
So by an unexpectedly early twist of fate
A young queen took on the heavy burden of state.

For sixty years, with Prince Philip at her side
To help, support and also often guide,
The Queen has travelled the globe, by land, sea and air,
Meeting people, leaders and monarchs everywhere.

Not every year has brought happiness and goodwill,
Her *'Annus Horribilis'* is remembered still,
But through it all her spirit had shone bright,
Even in times of depression it's a source of light.

Only one other monarch in the whole
Of British history has reached this goal,
The Queen's great-great grandmother, Victoria, of high renown
Achieved this especial landmark before passing on the crown.

So let us all send our congratulations
And join the Diamond Jubilee celebrations.
Wave the Union flags, let the banners be unfurled,
In honour of the finest sovereign in the world.

EILEEN BALLANCE

QUEEN ELIZABETH II – DIAMOND JUBILEE
(A CELEBRATION OF 60 YEARS OF SERVICE TO THE NATION AND THE WORLD)

Sixty years our Monarch of the British Isles,
Diamond Mother to the nation, with your warm
Royal smile. You've waved us through the good times;
Been steadfast when trouble passed, and with so much affection
We say – 'Thank you,' from our heart.

JOSIE MAY HODGES

OUR CENTURY

Jubilee, Jubilee, Jubilation!
Two diamond threads have woven through our nation
For sixty years ! – It's time for celebration . . .

We've walked this road apart – and yet together –
On sunshine days and through some rainy weather
Our century's evolved around us –
Since the twenties we've been totally amazed
How Man has overcome and culturally raised
Our country from despair and war
(Right back to when the British fought the Boer;
Then next with Kitchener's brutal war)

Into the thirties and the abdication
Uncertain times with Edward's resignation
Mapping *your* royal future at the age of ten
When thing would never be the same again

Courageous George then led his people through
An other war – with strength he never knew
Loved and respected up to nineteen-fifty-two

Your wedding day – November forty-seven
The match that truly has been made in Heaven
Dispelled out grey existence
Then the birth of Charles and Anne – but always Duty
Performed for sixty years with dignity and beauty

So – here we are! Survivors you and me
But you have on show for all the world to see
Your lifelong task fulfilled – and almost over . . .
We salute you Ma'am
And may you rest in clover!

EDNA SPARKES

Our Diamond Queen

She reigns supreme,
Our Diamond Queen,
She is loved by all
Whether short or tall.

She enjoys a joke
With friendly folk
And toes the line
In rain or shine.

During her holiday
So very far away,
She was called home
To sit on the throne.

Nineteen fifty-two
Was when she first knew
That her future home
Would be on the throne.

This year she was glad
To have had
A joyful time
With fellow Mankind.

Beacons were lit
On hilltops' summit
And fireworks thrown
For one person alone.

This local fun
Was for everyone,
But most for our Queen,
Who reigns supreme.

Kathleen White

MY REIGN

Now listen to me Blud -
Me is da Queen Liz.
Triumphant Monarch of Britain
'N' of da Commonwealth
U gets me?

Me seen lots of drama 'n' tragedies
Like a soap opera,
U know what I mean!
But I got through it all
Wid all my dignity
Philip wid me 24/7 is all I need -
Me bruvvas 'n' sistas all behind me . . .

Celebrities old 'n' happening,
Unsung heroes,
Prime Ministers 'n' Presidents
Have been welcomed
Through my humble abode.
And lots of stories
Have been bought 'n' sold!

It's been a long sixty years
But I won't give up yet –
Don't hold ur breath for nuttin' peeps
I've got heaps of strength
In every one
Of my old bones!

I'm going to celebrate my day
With great pomp 'n' style!
Gonna fill my cup with pink champagne,
So come wid me everyone
Cuz this day won't never come round again!

JAGDEESH SOKHAL

FOREVER LIKE DIAMONDS

We know that diamonds are forever
and we know well that we are safe
we will be safe till we're together
and diamond are our nights and days

We're not afraid the enemies
we have the inner strength to fight
and this strength come from our Queen
'cause her diamonds forever are

In these big days of celebration
let's make this promise for us all:
we'll be united as one nation
no matter if we rise or fall

God save the Queen and us – her servants
today, tomorrow and for keeps
please let us live the life we dreamt of
let our kingdom rest in peace

PIOTR BALKUS

REFLECTION

It's not the crown that captures my eye
As I look into the picture mirror.
Life's problems haven't passed me by
But turned my likeness into another.
Grey hair, solemn face, sag jaw and watered eyes
Belong to some ancient ancestor
Who reigned less long to my surprise.
Though thoughts inside sometimes pester
And, inward, on my internal mirror
A face emerges I know is my own,
Laughing, bright eyed with carefree manner,
In love with life and ruling none.
It's myself that the reflection amazes
And all the thanks and people's praises.

CHRIS ALLEN

GOD SAVE THE QUEEN

Don't Jubilieve it! That's what their posters say.
They have no Union Jack, *The establishment will pay!*

Pay for what I wonder?
For the bloodshot eyes and skeletal frame
That sits next door to their splendour?
They have ignored this drug-induced dame.

Or perhaps they want reimbursement
For their bed sheet and cat-black paint
Here I'll chuck them a fiver -
A real modern-day saint.

'I can see her! She's waving.' (Poor sod can only be six)
He doesn't know she's as powerless as he
The dame starts twitching for a fix.
'Down with the Monarchy, I am nobody's subject.
They're getting worked up now,
Hypocrisy takes years to perfect.

And as the carriage nears me, Drug Dame lifts an arm
A lone limb, drowning in flags – Will no one sound the alarm?

A crown and smile greets us,
How can they shout for her removal?
A sea of loyal subjects
And nine rebels for her perusal.

A wave is interrupted by shock and fear methinks,
She must have seen their posters, my own heart stops and sinks.

But she does not see their anger
Yet her face it hints at dread.
Her eyes are locked with Drug Dame's
A hundred sentiments unsaid.

The Monarch's paint is peeling, we witness warmth and feeling
The posters drop, protest a flop
And Drug Dame finally seen
Screams, laughingly, 'God Save the Fucking Queen!'

CHLOE MILLS

A FINE WAY TO RULE

When I think of all the changes her life has seen
And all the fabulous places that she has been
I do not feel jealousy, just deep admiration
For a woman who gives her life to the nation
With her head held high through many a trouble and strife
She is a daughter, a mother, a queen and a wife
Pride in our country is impossible to hide
For the die-hard royalists joy churns inside
Jubilee parties will fill many streets
Children playing games
As parents sing and tap their feet
Trestle tables down the middle of the road
As tales of the past begin to be told
At the tender age of 21, to London I did go
For the silver celebrations and a spectacular show
Tiny bits of paper floated down from the sky
As a very royal procession sedately passed me by
It is only whilst writing that I became aware
Of a large part of history the Queen and I share
I am so proud to be a part of her life and times
And the expansion of her family as well as mine
She keeps a level head through sadness, death and pain
I cannot visualise another royal to be the same.

LYNN ELIZABETH NOONE

62

ENGLAND

This land is England, are you mine or do you belong to another?
This decision is difficult for foreigners – whether England is our own country or not.

You, the monarch and your government belong to the English, but still you have provided a home for all of us foreigners.

Your ways are different and there is no other country that can compare to you.
You provide food, shelter and a means to live for all the asylum seekers.

You are recognised as a multicultural country. You provide jobs for all types of people and for all races.

You provide protection to all religions and provide justice to all Christians, Muslims, Hindus and Sikhs.

You do so much for us and still people think you are foreign to them. I do not understand why you do these things and favours for us.

In your free society you make us belong with so much love and affection and in such a way that it is hard for us, (foreigners), to forget this land.
It is difficult for me, (Asma), to decide which is our country – England or Pakistan?
The decision is difficult for us foreigners – whether England is our country or not.

NUZHAT ASMA CHAUDHRY

Congratulations Queen Elizabeth

Congratulations Queen Elizabeth,
It's your Diamond Jubilee!
60 years as sovereign ruler,
Hooray for the British monarchy!

On the night of June the 5th,
Your Dad King George sadly died,
Calm and composed in spite of your grief,
You filled his position with pride!

You and Philip were staying at Treetops,
When the tragic news came your way;
You climbed up a tree a Princess,
Came down a Queen the next day!

Your reign has not been easy,
Scandals have compromised your rule;
Shocking sensations in the news,
How on earth have you kept your cool?

You've been shown up by your family,
Their private lives in disarray;
Had to deal with pains in the ass,
Such as politicians day by day!

You've bravely toured the world,
Greeted crowds both in peace and war;
Stayed calm in the midst of riots,
Faced demonstrations and more!

Most impressing was when your calm control,
Of your horse, when bullets were shot;
And finding an intruder in your bed,
Even then you didn't lose the plot!

Serene and graceful through it all,
You have held your head up high;
You deserve a big celebration,
Millions of flags will fly!

On every house on every street,
Union Jacks and bunting will appear;
All young children will get a mug, A commemorative souvenir!

All of your subjects in Britain,
And well-wishers in every nation,
Apart from some anti-social miseries,
Will be partying for the occasion!

You deserve a medal for doing your job,
So hip hip hooray for you!
Wonderful horsewoman, steadfast Queen,
May you reign another century or two!

HELEN SILVERWOOD
2 KEEP FOREVER POEMS

RING OUT THE BELLS

Ring out the bells to chime, join in all the fun.
Long live our Diamond Queen who sparkles like the sun.
Sing along with love and joy for the sixty years she's served
In such a proud and happy way, celebrations are deserved . . .

Sixty years is quite a feat, such a lot of travel,
Meeting many, many types – how does she unravel?
Family Feuds – restless kids – she has known it all
And the countless times in life heads bang against a wall!

Our lives may not be quite the same, sixty years have left my feet
Not so used to travel, they're more like plates of meat!
As for family arguments, they are in the past,
The walls have dents to prove it, they weren't meant to last!
As for the diamonds, they're in Nature's glorious colours
And the occasional sparkling wine with a bunch of flowers!

Philip always by her side, dependable as always,
Happy, happy days,
Ring out the bells to chime, remember the dedication of sixty years,
Long may it continue even though in lower gears . . . !

M L DAMSELL

DIAMOND JUBILEE 2012

I'm writing a poem to celebrate,
The pride of our nation great,
So hoist up the bunting now,
And feel the good factor, wow!

Yes, on this auspicious day,
In glee we'll shout hooray,
The Queen's Diamond Jubilee,
Congratulations given cheerfully.

Glasses held high at a street party,
They say 'God Bless' to your Majesty.
As ancient bells across the land,
Give a signal to strike up the band!

Since the day of your Coronation,
Lovingly favoured by the nation,
And such changes you have seen
Since you became Great Britain's Queen.

We love to see you regularly
And wave our flags exuberantly.
As you travel past in motorcade,
To rule this land you surely made.

Across the nations of the world,
You are a marvel to behold.
For sixty years you have reigned,
From your service we have gained.

A stranger to me you are not,
Elizabeth, we love you a lot.
And that twinkle in your eyes,
Tells me, that's no surprise!

To your majesty we wish good health,
From the nation and the Commonwealth,
Your service given beyond compare,
Your Jubilee we are proud to share.

Because of you and the service given,
Our whole nation is globally driven.
To make the world a better place,
For members of the human race.

All nations perceive your Majesty,
As head of our great family,

Relationship built on shared history,
To this now add the Diamond Jubilee.

Close to us throughout your reign,
Not to compare in our lifetime again.
Our pride and joy whenever seen,
Witness our love for you our Queen.

And when all is said and done,
A Diamond Jubilee is a special one.
Your Majesty thank you for being true,
Elizabeth II, thank you for being you.

LUCY CAXTON BROWN

THE QUEEN'S DIAMOND JUBILEE

The beauties of a diamond reign, enclosures lure and longlasting,
Somewhat magical, somewhat wise,
With the intention of holding, clasping,
Classical gestures, Your Majesty, God save the Queen,
The Commonwealth,
The Commonwealth, there's more yet to be seen,
Glistening through, beyond, it's clearly fate,
You shine above with a beautiful imperial state,
No resigning, keep on track, it's where you're meant to be,
The Royal family, pleased and delighted on an occasion full of glee,
Times like this no more than ecstatic,
This is elegantly done with a palace by the side,
Doing well, relations thrive, ancestors watch and we abide,
We linger, leaping, ready to perceive,
In the Queen's eyes we believe,
Proud and willing, I pledge to you now,
A thousand more yet to vow.

HELEN RAMSAY

A DIAMOND JUBILEE SALUTE TO OUR QUEEN

With love and pride we salute our Queen,
For valiantly she had honoured each vow
Made before God, sixty years ago,
And has upheld them by faith even till now.

Anointed with the sacred oil,
She offered her heart, her mind and hands
To be dedicated to the service of God,
And to millions of people in all her lands.

She accepted the orb, affirming that
The whole world is ruled by Christ alone,
And promising that throughout her life
Christ would rule in her country and her home.

The sceptre and coronation staff
Meant justice and mercy would always flower.
The ruby ring placed on her hand
Bestowed royal dignity and power.

As St Edward's crown was placed on her head
The people cried, 'God save the Queen!'
Homage was paid by bishops and peers,
And the nation watched on the TV screen.

We thank You Lord for her service of love,
And in gratitude we humbly pray
That Your Holy Spirit will still inspire
And guide our Queen, this and every day.

DOREEN LAWRENCE

OUR QUEEN OF ENGLAND

Our Queen did she become in 1953, somewhat reluctantly may it sadly have been.
On her would history bestow the might of monarchy at Westminster, enthroned.
Amid the Abbey's hallowed splendour with crown and gown, orb an sceptre, this her majesty
she became . . .
So from that moment on to her duty she responded for Commonwealth
and England's Isles . . .
Amid a cheering crowd, shouting aloud, a thousand subjects her loyalty thus won . . .

Our Queen, then young at heart, her reign did start with a consort at her side . . .
Empire and Commonwealth, Principalities, would her devotion far surpass and outlast.
Other kings and queens would into history thus pass, our Queen, her stature growing.
Thus the years had flown by, her family now grown, betwixed loyalty and love shown.
Service before self, has she epitomised each November, always honouring the fallen.

Our Queen, let none deride, as brave souls bow, England salutes loyal subjects by her side.
Was their sacrifice in vain? She bears solemnly the Nations pain, long may she reign.
Can there ever be another such as she? Now approaching her Diamond Jubilee . . .
All her peers, has she thus far outshone, loyalty and duty as ever strongly arrayed.
Our Monarch and her England are but one, alas into history shall she pass, Queen and
country as one . . .
Three cheers, ma'am, well done, from your subjects of England, a beautiful land.

MICHAEL COUNTER

DIAMOND JUBILEE PRAYER

Cornerstone of this queenly realm,
Serenely dutiful, serving well
Her people of Great Britain and Commonwealth.

As we unite in joyful celebration of our Monarch's Diamond Jubilee
Let us thank God and pray for His continued blessing
Upon our Gracious Majesty.

Long live Elizabeth,
God save the Queen.

MALCOLM ANDREWS

The Diamond In Her Crown – Our Treasure

Come on, what is happening here.
It is very clear.
What a feeling.
Something awesome, fantastic, a'reeling.
There will be up and down UK and the world, parties on the street.
Good fellowship, food and a tapping of the feet,
The celebration of our Queen's Diamond Jubilee is at hand.
She has done so much for us over 60 years, representing our land.
Each year we eagerly listen to her speech,
Eloquent, meaningful and to us teach,
A curtsey we will send her as a pleasure
And to say, thank you dear Queen, the people's treasure.

Kathy Carr

2012 Diamond Jubilee

Her Majesty, relaxing in bed
With the crown perched on her head
Dreaming about her Diamond Jubilee.
There would be colourful streamers
Strung in all the towns and cities
In honour of her reign.
Marching up every hill we'll go
To light the beacon's fiery glow.
A boat on the river would be such fun
With cheering crowds in mid-morning sun.
Marching soldiers through the gate
Of Buckingham Palace, trying not to be late.
At the end of the day, when all would be quiet
Loads of bands will play a riot.
Now time to sleep to meet your dream
Of sixty years of being our Queen.

Oscar Smith

KINGDOM OF EXCELLENCE

The cool water of sea smoothed,
the sand the land complete.

As to champion the kingdom
gold silver and bronze as thought
as much to certain, the best of best because,

A canter in wonder on earth to define
'tween my thoughts is of nature's one course
of breeze of kind of wall force.

And as being to complementarity,
design in this time stands,
tangible, boundless
goals request, quintessence of our era.

A reach our bearing rein, of the greats
Excel and,
Peace equals, with excellence.

MICHAEL J WARD

THE SECOND ELIZABETH

Flags are gaily waving
In a sky of royal hue.
Such a diamond day
Rich in purple and blue.
Sixty years on the throne
Is celebrated in style.
Proud monarch of our times
Leading the rank and the file.

Let us join in jubilation,
One thought, one deed and one nation.

GWENDOLINE DOUGLAS

BESS

The fanfares played the trumpet blast
A Queen to serenade at last
The abbey's lined and filled with earls
And dames and duchesses all sporting pearls
And lords with ladies, dressed in style
Along that Coronation mile
A princess from a distant age, a princess who will rule our stage
That day in June, that day in time
Her role in history, that royal line,
Our London Queen, Our young Queen Bess
With hand and shoulders above the rest
That Hartnell dress, no lines, no crease
No shadows that the public sees
A train to stretch a million miles
Around the Abbey brings tears, brings smiles
This Tudor Rose, our Diamond Queen
That gold State Coach, this summer dream.

MICHAEL MAKIN

DIAMOND QUALITY

After shedding tears
For the loss of a father and loss of the girl
At a tender twenty-six years,
Her atoms have bonded with ours.
No cubic zirconia ruler – an industrial grade Queen,
At the highest end of the scale – flawless,
Unmoved by deep and stormy waters,
Shining strong with perfect lustre.
As Prime Ministers change with accompanying bluster
And while her corgis fight, she never lost sight
Of majesty and might.
In Greek diamond means unbreakable.
Like this matriarchal embrace is unshakeable.
After bullets, break-ins, crises, divorce,
Forever she remains, Elizabeth, of course.

KAREN BELL

CELEBRATIONS

I'm proud to be part of this country,
Our monarchy is something special.
We're rich, not only in our jewels,
The Queen will stand before us once again.

She has reigned for decades, it never ends, her honesty is true.
She shines out from the crowd, that's true.

Her elegance is honoured, her royalty is noble,
The emotion I feel when I look at her for real is admired by me
And my heart just reels from the history.

I stand, looking at the Queen gloriously,
Her jewels displayed, gleam brightly from the rays of the sunlight.

I stand tall the reflections, I'm in awe,
I'm proud to be in England, I'm connected to the core.

And so we all stand together once again,
We all have something to share,
As we put our hands together in celebration
For the Queen's Diamond Jubilee!

LIZ EVERETT

BRANDON HIGH STREET

Hello yer Madge, remember me?
I didn't think you would.
I am a subject, so you see
I've always been quite good.
Never broke the laws you passed,
Doffed my cap whenever asked.
I saw you once, you waved just so,
I waved too, not sure you know?
Brandon High Street, in the Rover,
You had stopped to let one over.
Sixty years is quite a blast,
You're working hard to make this last,
Knock old Vicky from the top spot,
Keep on going; do not stop.

MATTHEW HODDER

THE QUEEN'S DIAMOND JUBILEE

Behind her gracious smile
lie secrets of an Empire
Her family's achievements and qualms
displayed with unperturbed poise.
No frowning allowed
to spoil her regal face.
She held the reins of her kingdom for sixty years
with wisdom and compassion
and in this time or turmoil
let's hope she'll hold them steadily
for many more years to come
for everybody's sake.

NORIS D'ACHILLE

DIAMOND JUBILEE 2012

Much has been our pride
A gift of a lifetime our ride,
A royalty of heights so refined
Leaving the rest of the world behind

A wedding pageantry of 1947
Trooping the colour 1949
Coronation year 1953
Remembering my wedding also to be,
Colourful street parties making history
Showing the world freedom must be
Represented for all to see,
Royalty contrasting to
A disastrous world many pursue

June 2012 sees a Diamond Jubilee
And Olympic Games to turn the tide
Hosting many world wide,
Covering our shores
Sharing in the rewards,
Giving our Diamond Jubilee
Lasting hereditary.

BARBARA R LOCKWOOD

JUBILEE CELEBRATION DAY

In June of this year archangels will sing
As Diamond adds a glitter to gold,
Our devoted Queen of Commonwealth fame
Will have served sixty years on the throne.

Queen Elizabeth's true dedication
Includes many visits to countries afar,
Honours awarded to British people
And Royal Assents for acts above par.

Oh how we welcome her speeches
And her countenance sweetly divine,
The fifth day in June will be here very soon
When patriotic loyalty will shine.

JOYCE HEMSLEY

ELIZABETH OUR QUEEN

As she mourned the death of her beloved father,
She knew the role she was destined to take.
She had the happiness and the sorrow, through sixty years rule,
But she dedicated her life for our sake.

She has carried out duties at home and away,
Her love and dedication second to none.
With her husband beside her, with constant support,
Our hearts over the years she surely has won.

At Christmas her message is something we treasure,
As we watch and listen to her meaningful speech.
The love of family life outstanding all other
With thoughts of loved ones that cannot be reached.

We wish her good health and happiness,
Thank her for service over sixty years.
In this Jubilee year, our country's love surrounds her
With joyful celebrations and only happy tears.

MARGARET MEADOWS

HRH Queen Elizabeth II
Our Diamond

United Kingdom our family home,
Our Queen, a Mum to us all.
Welcomed people from other lands,
With equal opportunities through school!

Made friends with old enemies,
Through trade and communications,
Opened doors to love and friendship,
Harmony and warmth throughout the nations!

Always involved in fun and laughter,
Through the arts, drama, music and song!
Completely committed to the forces, children,
Hospitals, people so important, as all belong!

Always honoured and respected achievements,
Has curved traditions with progressive times!
The magic of having a modern Queen,
We can relate to Her in our lives!

She is our anchor in all state visits,
Has stood by Her government's decisions.
Hard times cut back Her own household,
Also invested money in our new visions!

Our extended family within the Commonwealth,
Proud too, the Queen is our diamond.
For we join hands in love and friendship,
Where prosperity and inspiration we share, goes on!

Ann Beard

QUEEN'S DIAMOND JUBILEE

2012 is our Queen's Diamond Jubilee
Elizabeth's been on the throne for sixty years
It's our British patriotic way to celebrate
By honouring her with bunting, parties and cheers

Will she beat her great gran's record?
Queen Victoria's sixty-four years long
If our Queen takes after her own mother
Her long, life will be as strong

So popular is our Queen
Long may she reign
With the marriage of Prince Wills and Kate
Many great grandchildren, heirs to gain

Wherever the Queen visits
The royal admirer's journey is worthwhile
When our Queen saw Norman Wisdom's famous trip
Her amusement was revealed with a big smile.

RITA WILDE

E R
(THE QUEEN'S DIAMOND JUBILEE)

Elizabeth of Windsor
Lynchpin of the realm
Spirit of Britannia
Heart and spear and helm
Orb and sceptre resting
In your guiding hand
Heralding New Glory;
Peace in every land.
This shall be your story
Till Time's last grain of sand.

BARRIE SINGLETON

LILIBET, OUR QUEEN

Lilibet when she was born
At her grandfather's house in Mayfair
Would never know the outcome
While later she became an heir

Her life was on a steady course
As the little life progressed
Her parents watched her closely
And each one was so impressed

Then came the day that Margaret was born
It meant so much to them all
These two little girls were happy
Everyone can recall

As Lilibet grew her young life was to change
As war reared its ugly head
Princess Elizabeth now to be known
Became a Subaltern instead

The years progressed for the princess
Elizabeth reached thirteen
It was then she met the man she'd marry
This young, impressive teen

On the 20th November 1947 she was married
To Philip once a Prince of Greece
Their love was there for all to see
They knew it would never cease

The events that followed were tragic
Her father, the king, had died
Elizabeth was to become Queen
Sadly the honeymoon ended for this young bride

The day of the Queen's coronation began
Her beauty enhanced her gown
Many had come from far and wide
And gasped when she wore her crown

'Hail Queen Elizabeth', rang out through the crowd
There were banners and flags flying high
No one could imagine what everyone felt
But I did see an odd tear in their eye

When the Queen and Prince Philip appeared from the palace
There was such a cacophony of sound
'God save the Queen' the crowd sang out
Their exultation was there to astound

The years have passed by and more changes are made
The Queen's Diamond Jubilee is here
The crowds will be here from all over the world
So good health to her Majesty and let's give her a cheer!

BARBARA FINCH

OUR DIAMOND QUEEN

Our Queen has reigned for sixty years
Very much loved and admired
Her lovely smile is genuine
Her stamina greatly desired
Other countries fight and destroy themselves
With unrest or violent reaction
While England runs smoothly in its own way
Without envy or dissatisfaction
We have our problems or financial woes
But try to rescue them with peace
Some former monarchs did not believe that
But our Queen wants war to cease
I would not like to live out of England
To me it's the best in the world
Having lived here in so many places
Finding nothing but goodwill unfurled
I am happy to have been born in this realm
Very glad that I live here in England
Grateful to have our good Queen at the helm
Giving us pride in our homeland.

MARY EAGLE

DIAMOND

Does it take 60 years to make a diamond?
And such a diamond.
One of strength and presence,
The loyalty to stay bright
And true through turmoil,
Change and decades past.
War and peace, and loss and life,
Strong, determined, diligent,
Loyal to her people,
Devoted to her family,
This diamond carries on.
A constant symbol to a country,
Very different from the one
She was crowned in.
So now we raise the bunting and
The flags, to remember and to
Wish her well, for long may
She reign over us.
Diamond Queen. Diamond Jubilee

GLYNNIS MORGAN

THE THRONE

The Queen on her throne must feel all alone
The Queen on her throne but she'll never moan
The Queen on her throne servants follow like drones
The Queen on her throne this is her home
The Queen on her throne bet she gives her dog a bone
The Queen on her throne it's all she's ever known
The Queen on her throne no one else she will loan

It must be tough, it must be hard, maybe boring, feel like snoring

The Queen on her throne for 60 years –
Joy, sadness, maybe some tears

We celebrate it, she will too
But what happens if she needs the loo?

JULIE GIBBON

THE QUEEN'S CORONATION

Westminster Abbey in 1953
An important part
Of our whole history
We were lucky to share
The Queen's Coronation
Televisions ablaze
With dignitaries, elation
She was beautiful composed
We were so proud that day
There were huge celebrations
With all the display
Everyone shared street parties
With bunting and flags
With music and dancing
Cakes, sandwiches and lemonade
A day of rejoicing
The greatest of days
To end all the magic
Our new Queen appeared
On the balcony of the palace
Where the whole country cheered
As proud as could be
With Prince Philip by her side
She was now crowned our Queen
And Prince Philip's new bride

JEANETTE GAFFNEY

THE DIAMOND YEAR OF OUR QUEEN

Tolling, tolling bells ring,
Loud and clear for our Queen.
A sea of flying flags
And children, all smiling in the street.
Dancing to catchy
Tunes and lively feet,
Bars filled with the sound of laughter,
Drinks hold Jubilee full of joy and rapture,
Thank God for her long reign!

SAMMY MICHAEL DAVIS

OUR DIAMOND QUEEN

In sixty years
you have lead us Ma'am
by your reign
of dignity and calm
through all the wars
terrors and fears
you have steered us safe
for sixty years
we can only imagine
how hard it has been
to remain so calm
so loyal, so serene
but you have shown a strength
so rarely seen
that makes you Ma'am
our Diamond Queen.

DAPHNE CORNELL

ELIZABETH

Such elegance and grandeur has,
demure and delicacy divine
enchantment is her beauty thus – beguiling.

Her smile such sensuous delight,
captivating in her loveliness,
so fresh her spirit ever dwells – sublime.

In majesty she reigns supreme,
unequalled in her beauteousness,
delightful, charmingly she rests – appealing.

Enchanting, temptingly assured,
by gracious Heavenly command,
has loyally guarded o'er this realm – this England –
thank you Ma'am.

HANNAH R HALL

THE DIAMOND ON THE THRONE

When a diamond rests on
roses, red and white,
with the gild of a thousand
lights, stolen from the stars of night.
And be like a candle
whose flames splinters shadow,
and be the grass that
winds truth in the meadow.
With strings of a heart held
by a many hands,
that same heart that guides
the hands through shadows over lands,
and leads into the radiant sun,
the thousand blooms of admirers,
as a phoenix reigns in a glorious light
from the flames of regent fires.
And by the roars of a lion
that sings not alone
and with such a gilded crown
a Diamond stands on a royal throne.

ANNA-LOUISE RAINFORD

60 YEARS

The past 60 years have to have been seen to be believed.
Black and white sets replaced by plasma 3Ds.
The landline phone has turned into a wafer handheld machine.
James Bond-like contraptions everywhere to be seen.
Phone books made redundant as the google trend appears.
Non-edible Oysters replace the faithful Red Rovers
And the top of double-deckers are no longer for the smokers.
Typewriters, vinyl recorders now a thing of the past,
MP3s and downloads replacing them fast.
Deaths, births and marriages, happiness and dreams,
(Not always as you'd hoped they would be)
Nevertheless, all part of life's rich pattern,
The past 60 years have to have been seen to be believed.

JOSEPHINE MARIE DE CERA

JUBILEE

English St George's crosses, bond with Welsh emblem dragons
Irish and Scottish royal kisses, flagships flown by well wishers
Sea of faces, 3D animation, picture jigsaw depicting a nation
Union Jacks sway in waves of patriotic undulation
A rainbow spectrum of brollies ready, on call
For this is a British June midsummer's day after all

An island, consolidated, not in protest, strike or in riot
Diamond Jubilee celebration, Queen and country congregation
The wrinkled, painted, dimpled, sticky-faced and pimpled
Multi-faith, multi-lingual, multi-cultures all intermingle
No ageism, racism or gender discrimination
No political, radical agenda, just happy joining of nation

The lawyer, lorry driver, teacher, mortgage advisor
Grandad, neighbour, brother, stranger, friend, single mother
Alfresco city picnics, sandwiches, cake and hot drinks
Anticipation, expectation, hours spent patiently waiting
Respect, admiration for monarchy, duty, crowned on her
But to unite fractured kingdom what an extraordinary honour

SHIRLEY CLAYDEN

DIAMOND JUBILEE

53 nations make our British Commonwealth,
the best the world had ever known.
Where Queen Elizabeth, our British Queen
across the world she is renown.
For freedom, fairness and intellect
my Queen is like a granite stone
and speaks from her heart, like it should be,
with a smile that would shatter any stone.
So, on June 2nd 2012, your Diamond Jubilee,
I wish you all the very best my friend
and all your family.

JOHN HICKMAN

DIAMOND JUBILEE

I recall the Jubilee of 1977
And no opening up of the heavens
We all dressed up and had a ball
With a wig and glasses, I was the youngest granny of them all.
A big street party with loads of food
My dad filming the frivolities and mood.

Do I really remember? I was only five
It is the cine film that keeps the memory alive?
So after sixty years of British reign
Which pic, Liz do you think is the correct vein?
To encompass your life throughout the years
Thousands of photos yielding varying sentiment, hopes and fears.

1952 Liz was crowned
what's our Queen encountered while around?
No strangers to scandals, the royals
And through the media we get the spoils.
So what do we really know of our Queen?
After sixty years of reign, what do you glean?

Sixty-five years ago she married Phil
Both still going strong, no sign of 'past it' or 'over the hill'
Regularly seen in the arena of public domain
Longevity and love, licked, long may she remain.
Our monarch a stalwart and always with Phil by her side
Ever supportive, loving and many a laugh I'm sure he provides.

I like the fact she's a mum and a gran
Again, she couldn't do that without her man.
Yeah, a strong union was formed when Phil took Liz as his wife
To share and shoulder the experience of life.
Sixty-five years married is an achievement alone
Without mentioning the sixty years on the throne.

And we are invited to celebrate the Diamond Jubilee
With our friends, loved ones and families.
Do it, share a sense of community, makes Britain great
Be proud of our royalty and celebrate
And don't forget when you raise your drinking arm
To say congratulations on your 60 years Ma'am.

DONNA GIBLIN

Celebrations And Congratulations

Up and down the country
Different events are being planned
To celebrate Queen Elizabeth's Diamond Jubilee
Arrangements are in hand

There will be many street parties
Trees planted and beacons lit
Lots of towns and villages
Will celebrate as they see fit

In July we have the Olympics
Featuring lots of well known names
Good luck to all the participants
Involved in these famous games

What a busy year for Her Majesty
As she travels near and far
Meeting with her public
Or waving from her car

So I'll raise a glass to you Ma'am
And give three hearty cheers
Sincere congratulations to you
On sixty glorious years.

Jackie Richardson

FROM A PAUPER TO A QUEEN
(A PARCEL)

If towards your bedroom this parcel drifts,
Open it without fear, it is a gift.

A diamond melted into lines on paper;
'Tis the family heirloom of a pauper.

Borrowed the envelope; I had no seal,
Pardon me, my saliva glued it still.

With my wishbone in hand I watched it drift
Over waters, mountains and valleys rift.

Just to utter this simply, 'I commend you
For sixty years of reign Queen Lizzie Two.

'Tis sixty years of UK made dynamic;
Your positive vibrations are pandemic.

God save the Queen, God save Europe's fluorescence;
The quintessence of colossal eminence.

Last night I saw with drowsy eyes
Your constellation forming in the skies.

This morn my gift is a melted diamond,
On paper, to soothe your heart and beyond.

So if towards your heart this parcel drifts;
It's not a letter bomb, it is a gift.

RAYMOND UYOK

REMEMBERING

The last sixty years
They reign in my mind
This is the way that they sparkle
To the unfortunate blind
I remember the deaths
We've faced the wars
Of hip new generations
And settling old scores
Battling with technophobes
And heading towards today
It hasn't been easy
But England's found a way
And sixty years on
As the diamond memories rust
The remnants of past lives
Are no more than dust
Yet they live on
Through images revisited and re-seen
And we use our future
To enlighten us where we have been.

LAURA SALMON

ELEGANT

Like our Queen I find many people extremely funny,
I've four children like her and try not to carry money.
Here similarities end; I do not have personal maids,
If I decide to take a day off work, I won't get paid.

Her Majesty is a great grandma and I am one too!
Often she wears suits of various colours, I prefer dark blue.
I like her style, an elder lady who can do elegant,
As a fashion icon she is notorious, a giant.

On only one point she stalls, in height she is very small,
Not that this fact has been a stumbling block at all.
At her magnificent age life is really busy,
But I enjoy relaxing times with cake and cups of tea.

SUSAN MULLINGER

EBB, TIDE AND FLOW

Through war and peace
catastrophe
and family trauma
her Majesty
has reigned supreme
an anchor of stability
amid the governing classes.
In this, her
Diamond Jubilee year
the monarchy
sails in calm seas
with public acclaim
in cheers and waves.

Its heritage and pageantry
are world-renowned
and all involved
should be justly proud
with the Queen at the helm
to fulfil their role
with dignity and dedication.

Long may she reign
and those who follow
in her wake
sustain with her passion
the tide and flow
of public support
to triumph in survival.

In contrast
Our political elite
are at a low ebb
from shady dealings
over the last decade
and a world now in
financial disarray
steered by a bonus culture.

ROBERT FALLON

CORONATION DAY PLUS TWO

Sixty years ago when
I was just ten
Elizabeth was crowned Queen
And I was amongst the cheering crowds to be seem.
We stood row upon row on the hill
Balloons, streamers and bunting did the air fill.
Excited and patiently we waited
Then the sound of horses' hooves drew near,
There was a ripple of applause and then a mighty cheer
'Long live the Queen,
God save the Queen!'

Waving flags held in tiny hands,
Many a youngster on parents' shoulders stand,
Along came the carriage, along came the band,
Passing us lucky ones in the grandstand.
I was happy I had patiently waited,
In that carriage sat a royal,
A lady, with a crown upon her head
And precious jewels sparkling in the sunlight,
Wearing an ermine cloak edged in white,
Waving to her loyal
Subjects, whose voices in unison rang
'God save our gracious Queen,
Long live our noble Queen,
God save our Queen!'

Then the cheers and church bells rang
Out; all too soon the procession had passed by us
I felt a tiny tear in my eye,
My mother wiped it away
And for many a day
Those magical words rang in my ears,
'Long live the Queen,
God save the Queen!'

PATRICIA J TAUSZ

MEMORIES OF OUR QUEEN

Thoughts of you brings memories new
To reality
Of life
I've watched you grow and bloom
I've even laugh with you
I've seen and heard your voice
With or without choice
I've cared with you
And cried with you
Been proud of you
And mad with you
In your sixty years of reign
I've seen positivity
With endless possibilities
Creativity
Using your mind to rule
And help Mankind
A special strength in a voice
When you have had no choice
Battles you've won
In the mystery of life
The choice is yours and ours
Giving strength, making others stronger
When tomorrow has meaning
And days have hope
With passion you touch us so soft
And true
Amazing woman are you
60 years we celebrate
Through good and bad, happy and sad
We have seen
You, our Queen
Of the country
God bless you
In all you do.

LINDA BEVAN

DIAMOND JUBILEE

In February nineteen fifty-two, Elizabeth came to reign,
she flew back from overseas and stepping from the plane
was met by Winston Churchill to be England's young, new Queen
and through the years has proved to be the best there's ever been.

Age twenty-six, you showed the world the way it should be done,
with charm and glamour on your side, the nation's hearts you won.
You moved to Buckingham Palace where for sixty years
you've been,
know as the House of Windsor, it's the place fit for our Queen.

Sixty years you've reigned and ruled, consistent through and through
and I know our nation would agree when I say may God bless you.
I praise your dedication and admire your zest for life,
head of the British Commonwealth, plus a mother and a wife.

To commemorate your sixty years as our well established Queen,
they're going to put a concert on the best we've ever seen,
it's to be outside the palace front and all down through the Mall
and when asked will we enjoy it, you bet your life we shall.

Gary Barlow's been appointed to plan this one-off scene
and nothing but the best will do for our special Diamond Queen.
We have the greatest pop groups and musicians known to man,
presented with the style and flair that only Britain can.

With six decades to chose from, all the music will be ace,
there'll be something on for everyone in the entire human race.
We'll see Sir Cliff and Elton and Sir Paul McCartney too,
Dame Shirley and Tom Jones as well, to mention but a few.

But although it's made in Britain, no doubt the world will see
and that's because we'll tune in to your Diamond Jubilee.
It won't be just fantastic, or outstanding and unique,
It'll be the envy of all Mankind, from the States to Mozambique.

It's hard to write down into words your sixty-year crusade,
that's packed with great achievements of the kind that never fade.
You've earned your place in history; and the writing's on the wall,
as Head of State you've done us proud, you're the greatest of them all.

I therefore now salute you, on your well-earned Diamond Day,
I pray your hopes and expectations are fulfilled in every way.
It'll be a scintillating time for all, so enjoy it come what may,
which leaves me just one thing to say – and that's have a
brilliant day.

PHILIP BOOTE

BELLS RING, CHEERS ROAR FOR A SPAN OF THREE SCORE

Sixty years our sovereign has ruled the country by way of hereditary tradition,
Since changing circumstance occurred and made an appointment to the crown,
Over this duration Her Royal Highness has grown in wisdom and stature
Dedication to the role as Queen has earned respect and worldwide renown.

Great Britain is governed by a Monarch, dignified, poised, cultivated, erudite
Even following lengthy flights, train, road journeys is perfectly collected, polite.
Commonwealth visits, demanding tours, schedules, contrasts of chill and heat
Occasional breaks must provide relief when engagements are all complete.
Consistently the welcoming smile, ever present, dominates each proceeding
Video coverage shows you in control, newspapers make interesting reading.

I was four years old when the coronation was broadcast in nineteen fifty-three
My parents did not own a TV but kind neighbours said, 'Call here and see'
Recollection includes a golden carriage, flags waving, such a thrilling sight,
Being young, meaning was not grasped and pictures were in black and white.
Style of ceremony remains, links today with reminiscence down memory lane
Personal reflection adds sentiment to this grand celebration of historic reign.

In every family challenges arise, but Her Majesty endures, adherent to duty,
Informal gatherings allow humour, warmth of personality, affable, not snooty.
Prince Philip had been a rock, quoted often for saying precisely what he thinks
He is greatly admired for overseeing, an indomitable spirit that never sinks.

To mark this Diamond Jubilee, a magnificent flotilla will sail down the Thames,
Just think, Royal Yacht Britannia could appear as one of its glittering gems!
(Plus its welcome respite from squabbles of Labour, Tories and Lib Dems)
A majestic scene to witness, adding to our maritime episodes, links with water
Fine tribute to a well loved, popular King and consort's praiseworthy daughter.
An earlier festival when the master, Handel, composed his aquatic dedication,
Provided a spectacle and his fireworks were aglow in sparkling sensation.

Representatives from all nations will send congratulations and best wishes
As toasts, lubricated with champagne, are accompanied by exquisite dishes
Souvenirs, DVDs and memorabilia on offer will capture for posterity record
A rich heritage of pageant, continuity, stability, plus long service award.

In modern times with lowering standards and corruption leading folk astray,
We require strong example, principles, moral guidelines to illuminate the way.
Following this unique event, hope, goodwill, unity, community, favour resides,
To build a future, prosperous, enlightened, noble, where true fellowship abides.

DENNIS OVERTON

A ROYAL PROGRESS

Jubilee hits our thoughts once more
Bringing back recollections of royalty and renown
Painted in skilful detail on eye-catching memorabilia
With inscriptions irrevocable and timeless
Dated as precious accolades

Gifts stored in china cabinets and display cases
After purchase from promotional retail stores
A permanent reminder of a royal occasion
When eye-catching posters graced the metropolis
And colourful, bustling street parties
Were the order of the day

Yet glancing to the past
Focussing on momentous moments of history
Consider how streams of time and activity flowed
Since the historical coronation

Recalling the event's fervour so well;
As we approach
The renewed spotlight directed at the publicised elegance
Of her golden commemorations

Picturing events after her ascent
In various scrutinised poses

Royals rapidly dying, marrying, reuniting
All in a frantic rush of years
Jostling for positions
Like players in a game
Risking prison for a cause
Facing menaces of warzones

Faces so insensitively, professionally photographed
Without protection of privacy
Splayed so frequently across the tabloids
Or hounded by paparazzi
Then vanishing into palaces
Or periodic silences

Talking point in press office
Slanderous truths

Such obtrusive propaganda
'Everybody knows
What there is to know'

About the supposed royal privileges
No curtailed liberties involved
At all

Still our Queen hangs in there
Eternally
Still gracing our screens at Christmas
Ready to face her new era
Even when facing
Rigours of sophisticated age

Let's hope her Jubilee
So soon forthcoming
Proves to be impactful
Causing England to move ahead
Progressing from present recessionary malaise and chaos
As she appears
Such a newsworthy leader
Head maybe to be outlined in discrete detail
On updated twenty-first century coinage
New images
Soon decorating royal showcase
And attracting public purse

So much more experienced
Than on her glorious Coronation Day
With her assumption of regal power
Many decades ago

Coronation to Jubilee
Proved a chequered unpredictable journey
A century or so elapsed
Resulting in amelioration
Or imminent disaster!

What price fame?

Question the media will soon solve
As government wallow in allegations of double dealing
And she must once again
Rush to face the listening crowds
Undeterred
By the publicity machine
On her Jubilee Day

TRACY ALLOTT

LETTERS TO THE QUEEN

As a rebellious child, I knew nothing of life, death and the bits in-between.
I was too busy making catapults, bows 'n' arrows, fishing for 'taddies' in the beck.
What the heck did it all mean 'The King is dead, long live our Queen?
I'd never seen either of 'em except on the picture screen.
Mum said, 'Bless him, he's gone. Passed away.'
No idea the importance of that. Passed where? Had he gone on a trip to Scarbro'
for the day?
We all cramped into Mrs Naylor's best room to watch the beautiful Princess Elizabeth crowned
Queen, on a nine inch TV screen,
Then it dawned on me, how regal she was.
Mum said, through tear-filled eyes, 'She'll reign supreme.'
The years followed as I mellowed and had my own family.
Our beautiful Queen cares for is without a throne!
My beloved mother, a true royalist and best friend too
Mary Whitehouse wrote to both, rather too much,
Complaining of how the miners, (her brothers), were being treated like muck, of how our
nation would fall into decline
As mine after mine closed, how cruelty to animals and neglect of children left her indisposed.
Christmas was the highlight of Mum's year.
After lunch we would raise our glasses,
'To our Queen, God bless her!'
Hungover teenage grandsons, full to busting, with adults, worn out mum, glued to the oven
raised another
'God bless you and yours, from one mother to another'
This celebratory year of her putting on a brave face for sixty years,
Makes me proud to have been part of it all.
My eldest son is fifty, the Olympiad and Diamond Jubilee.
What a wonderful year this will be.

JOYCE HEFTI-WHITNEY

THE TIME WAS RIGHT

The time was right for you to be Queen
everyone knew you would reign supreme.
Always duty first and your people's welfare
it shows you are a true Queen
and really care.
For you your people will always be there
to cheer you on through thick and thin
whether you lose or win.
You are a real lady amongst the fray
from your people you will never stray
for this reason they love you alone
yours is always the throne
of true love and justice.

ELIZABETH PHILLIPS SCOTT

UNTITLED

She was young
She was innocent
She was free

She became trapped
She became a leader
She became Queen

Her father to be king . . . a stroke of luck
Her a queen . . . destiny!

She is a diamond
She is a Diamond Queen.

REBECCA STINTON

THE JUBILATION OF OUR QUEEN

There's going to be a celebration
All about our great and gracious Queen
It's going to be a jubilation
One we have never seen

Her Majesty was just a young girl
When she became our Queen
Her mind must have been in quite a whirl
Knowing what it would mean

Her life would be taken over
With traditions and wordly things
And would her true love and new husband
Wonder if this would change things?

But they soldiered on together
They had bad and good times to bear
But true love lasts forever
And now they have the Jubilee to share

The queen wants all the people
To join in this celebration year
And what great things we can do
To make it great for her

So hang the flags and balloons for HRH to see
For most of us the same age as the Queen
Won't live to see another Jubilee.

KATHY FRENCH

DEAR ELIZABETH,

It has been a long time, hasn't it?
You look well, less stern, more friendly;
each endured throughout the years.
It feels OK to address you so, but
never before during troubles,
when my grandfather felt the anger
and humiliating ways of rubber bullets.
No pantheon could ever quell his purpose,
truths he shared with me,
these became my arteries of belief,
from such a young age.
He is no longer, like many of his way.
I wonder how these days would stack for them?
My craw has lost that lump; dissolved,
ears listen in more understanding ways,
heart and mind lives in present day
hope, though older, different eyes.
This may not sit well with many,
perhaps one day it will.
I have learned of a new place to view
from soul, to cogitate in different fields,
while history holds its station,
you understand,
for more peaceful ways.
Mise le meas,

MICHAEL BRACKEN

CHEERS

We unroll bunting
And set the scene.
An excuse for a party,
It's the Queen's Jubilee.

Sixty years is our toast,
Countless days as our host.
Always smiling as she's giving
And travelling near and far.

She can say a hi on Facebook
And Tweet a quick hello.
A familiar face in many ways,
Though how the times have changed.

Ask any child, of any age,
They know that smile,
Those hats, that wave.

Yet those many hats
Are worn, like us,
A mum, a nan,
A wife and more.

So lift a glass
And say a toast,
Here's to sixty good years,
May she reign many more.

NICOLA WILLIAMSON

THE ARIADNE THREAD

Last night I came across a poem in my father's old poetry book,
the one by Ellie Nelligan, valiantly propped up
between pages fifty-four and fifty-seven
and boldly entitled Christ on the Cross.
And there, on the upper right corner, a crease
(marking the page so carefully folded so long ago)
gave pause to reflection –
a respite as eyes wandered on the words that had been sketched
like a train of letters rippling through time.
And, as I imagined a plaster Christ, crumbling alabaster,
a Marmo di Castellina lovingly rendered by some obscure artist,
I found myself quite inexplicably holding my breath
for fear of diluting an agony that had been
crafted amongst the stanzas and phrases flowing in my father's mother tongue.
Mouthing the words in silent revelry,
This poem, idolized as once uttered by someone dearly loved and missed,
Tenderly invited contemplation on the message
of suffering and impending death
of hope and deliverance
referenced like the heavy fragrance of lilacs on a hot summer's night
and embodied in the nuances of a whispered prayer.

Continuing to read
I slowly gathered the courage to peer within
this poet's touch, conveyed an Ariadne thread
and imagined my father's emotions
as he read those same words so long ago.

J D R BEAUDOIN

The Gems That Sit Upon The Diamond

The jewels that rested upon her shoulders
Were never quite so grand
As the man she would grow old with,
Who will remain at her right hand
To stay beside her throughout her time
And help her govern all the land.

The golden carriage that she took
Could never outshine
Her children's shining looks as
She continually defined
The past sixty years on the throne
As Our Majesty, so fine.

The gems that sat upon the diamond
Glowed not nearly as bright,
As the eyes that lay beyond them
When they turn and reunite
With her people and their smiles
That form at her regal light.

L A Cooper

Raise A Glass

What can we do to show our love and respect?
Are we sure you can hear us and see us?
We can sing the Anthem and loudly proclaim,
'Send her victorious!'
and know by the zeal
that it's a good send off.
We can clink glasses and listen to a louder mouth say,
'Hip hip hooray!'
Your day is truly our day
and we will raise a glass and older fans of yours
will wipe tears on facial tissues.
Gripping our carnival flags we affirm our pride in you
and listen for the second verse to start;
'God save our gracious Queen.'

Gillian Lawrence

NOT JUST A QUEEN – A ROYAL LEGEND

Not just a Queen but a friend to all of her people
At her coronation her pride was higher than the cathedral steeple
To serve and to care for her country was her desire
Her determination glowed like an ongoing fire
She has reigned sixty years and we hope she will still go on
She is so determined, very willful and so very strong
A beautiful lady, with a strong family trend
She will always care for her people right up to the end
For she thinks of us all with the highest accord
Not only in England but in our countries abroad
She makes time to visit her people and show her care
And always makes sure that she has time to share
To shake hands and to chatter, she will not pass you by
She wouldn't make anyone unhappy or see them cry
Her people all love her, Prince Philip, her children and grandchildren too
But now, as sixty years have gone by, yes, sixty years on the throne
She is still happy for the palace to remain as her home
So we wish you, Your Majesty, a happy anniversary, a happy day
Please enjoy every moment and all good wishes in every way.

PATRICIA MAYNARD

JUST A DAY

The Queen's Coronation gave us a day off school
I remember it, like it was yesterday
the snag was we had to watch it on telly
thank God we were let out to play.

We were given a mug and book to remember
yet how could one forget?
A day when the Earth stood still
and all seemed perfect and set.

It's a catalyst, a snapshot in time, like
a peg to fasten things on
of a time and a place that was special, but past
for that day, so real, is gone.

ROBERT SHOOTER

JUBILEE JUBILANTY

Red, white and blue are the colours on view
Our gracious Queen, Elizabeth the Second
is worthy of this hue,
Her sixty years of glorious and faultless leadership
we give her due
Through times of austerity and plenty,
we passed through not a few.

This June we join the crowds cheering, hip hip hooray
On our happy and most auspicious very special day,
She has surely shown the perfect and right way
What enemies we may have had have
surely been kept at
bay.

The flags will come out and the bunting as well
We will all have a good time, our offspring later to tell,
Playing the royalty card never fails to ring the bell
All colours and backgrounds never ceasing to yell.

As the crowds gather, hailing from Land's End
to John O' Groats
We shall yell, God save the Queen, with a lump in our throats,
If she were up for election she could count on my vote
But alas I am a commoner and no one of note.

She has reigned over us through bad times and good
Though people regard me as a stick in the mud,
I'd like to do something special if only I could
But in Her Majesty I see nothing but good.

As the years speed past we look back into history
And the part played by Elizabeth 1st,
Victoria shrouded in mystery,
But my God and hers has shaped our destiny
Having ruled country and commonwealth
well down to her excellency.

The years have sped past and it's destined to last
The die has been cast and our colours fly proudly
from the mast,
We show our appreciation to our monarch,
our devotion is vast
Shouting in harmony, 'God save the Queen
and stand back aghast.

JOHN WABY

THE QUEEN'S JUBILEE

The Queen of England must often reflect on the years she has reigned
Through wars, poverty and family conflictions
The Queen has shown, with unfailing strength
Her duty to this country, her subjects and personal triumph

What do you think goes through her mind
As she celebrates her Diamond Jubilee?
Is she happy, wanting to rest or will continue to the end
As she first set out as a young lady with the world at her feet?

People will be celebrating, in towns, cities and countries
We even get given the day off, which adds to the appeal
To join in or relax at home with a homely slap-up meal

The Queen, Her Majesty, we salute you
For giving this country their prestige
Of the Royal Family and Buckingham Palace
And all the excitement of the Diamond Jubilee

CLAUDETTE CARBY

A MORNING IN JUNE, REMEMBERED

Sunrise over the Thames
A proud and jubilant London awakening
To the sound of horses' hooves
In the distant mist.

A trembling excitement rushes through
The crowd
At each sound, at each movement,
Each sight of the gathering throng.

Then, in a breathtaking, sudden moment,
The Golden Coach sparkles past them
Like a dream,
The young and beautiful Queen about to
Dedicate her life to her people.

Waving to them, they,
Awestruck by the majesty of the occasion,
With one voice utter
A loud and beautiful cry,

'God Save the Queen.'

JUDY ROCHESTER

Queen's Diamond Jubilee

Our Queen has ruled for sixty years
with untiring dedication,
Through the challenges that life presents
she remains loyal to her nation.
The vows she took in '53
were made with heart sincere,
And as her reign progresses
she is loved more each and every year.
I sometime pause and ponder
if I ever have the chance
How would I cope with royal duties,
all the pomp and circumstance.
I could handle having servants
to attend to mundane chores
Like cleaning all the windows
or hoovering all the floors!
To have my own designer
to make outfits of my choice,
With matching hat and shoes and bag
oh how I would rejoice.
But the monarch's 'job description'
requires dignity and grace
Could I smile quite regally
whatever time or place?
Would I be bored at shaking hands
with the hundreds that I meet,
And how would I disguise the fact
that I had aching feet?
Could I appear quite interested
when the PM comes to call
to speak of stately matters,
no, it would drive me up the wall!
If I felt the sudden urge one day
to pop down to the shop
I could not just put on my coat
and wait at the nearest bus stop.
Thus, to our much loved Queen Elizabeth,
whom you never hear complain,
Although I could not do your job
a loyal subject I'll remain.

I'll be dressed up proudly
to wave my flag with glee,
Attired in colours, red, white and blue
on your Diamond Jubilee.

DOREEN COOK

HISTORY AND TIME

Born in the mid 1950s, how time has flown
As in history and I have watched, learned and grown
As time and I evolved
Conflicts of wars tragically rose and resolved
The first man to walk on the moon
Concorde aircraft breaking the sound barrier's boom
The invention of Texas instruments, LED watch and calculator
Fantastic changes for an aircraft aviator
Black and white TV to colour remote TV, with digital surround
Mono to stereo, to digital sound
From a vinyl record to tape and CD to DVD and MP3
To technological advances from a mechanical binary machine
To ever-growing PC
From Alexander Graham Bell to text sent on a mobile phone
From pesticide uses to cell developed clone
Cooking on a stove to microwave
Energy efficient devices that save
A letter put in the post
Email sent through a network host
All these things in my short life I've seen
Passed through history have come and been
The rule of one Queen and her Silver Jubilee
My Highness, Elizabeth is the monarch I see
What more marvels does history hold in store
In the future opening its door?

TERRY JOHN POWELL

A BLESSED SOUL

Dear Her Majesty, God bless your soul to reign over England,
Christ gave you wisdom and long life to rule justly over your blessed people.

Let your light continue to shine as you live and reign like a blooming flower smiling in the kisses of the shimmering rain.
The soft touch of the wind shall guide your heart like a ship that's drifted slowly in the serene sea to reach her ultimate destination.

Live and soar like the eagle into the skies some day and watch your kingdom grow like a verdant garden among the hibiscus flowers that smile and dance at the break of dawn in summer's heat.

Give your heart to Jesus, He will direct your path in the heat and cold and when your earthly life shall come to an end you shall sing praises to God in the highest heaven far away,
Where angels worship God and sing divine songs from eternity to eternity.

Remember you are just an instrument of God to rule and reign upon this Earth, guided like King Solomon by the divine hands of God.

May your soul expand in the divine ocean of wisdom from eternity to eternity, where your name will be remembered by great and small and you shall live forever,
immortalised by fame.

Your life is like a dream that appears in our sleep then you are gone like the wind when your mortal vessel shall be broken, you shall take your leave to live in God's divine mansion from eternity to eternity just as the sun rises at dawn and is gone at sunset into the west, so shall you be like the rains hidden in the curtain of the clouds.

What is your life dear Majesty but a divine spark from Jesus who guides your soul to rule and reign for sixty years.

Live forever more until you fly away like an eagle through Heaven's golden door.

GIDEON SAMPSON CECIL

QUEEN'S DIAMOND JUBILEE

The Queen's Jubilee
Takes place in June
What a day that will be
For millions of people
Like you and me
Revered by all
She can walk tall
Her exemplary style
Is a shining example
That stands out a mile
Her keen sense of duty
For all – high or low
So different
To those days long ago
How fortunate we are
To have such a 'star'
May she carry on longer
And grow ever stronger
Come June we'll be
Over the moon
We shall stand
And rejoice
Saluting you Ma'am
Singing and shouting
'God bless our Queen.'

MARTIN SELWOOD

HMS Vanguard 1953

It was in the month of June, the year 1953
I know that was a long time ago
But that's twixt you and me,
Almost sixty years ago
My own Diamond Jubilee,
I remember very well that visit
By Her Majesty the Queen
It was choreographed to perfection
A most engaging scene.

Why, may you ask should memory serve me thus?
It was the first time I'd been addressed by Royalty
And it caused an awful fuss.
I remember Her Majesty looking up into my eyes
(She is quite a small sovereign)
I mean small that is, in size.

With a hint of a Mona Lisa smile
Playing about her lips
She said and I must confess
In a sort of stage whisper
'You are standing on my dress.'
Well! My toes involuntarily curled up
Within my size nine shoe
Thus removing the weight and releasing
That gown of azure blue.

She acknowledged the guard of honour
With a gracious, knowing smile
Her eyes lingered upon me
For what seemed and eternal while.
Well, I did not know whether to blush or f**t
In fact I did both, unwise
Well not being allowed to speak
I could hardly apologise.

That was not my last meeting with Her Majesty
Our paths were to cross again
I made sure my size nines kept out of reach
Of her gown and that damned train.

LOYD DAVID BURT

ST EDWARD'S CROWN

If I may be so bold to break, your Majesty,
my golden silence of these threescore years,
I don't get our much Ma'am, will never see
Royal Ascot, Epsom Derby, hear crowds' cheers,

no walkies with the Labradors. It galls
that drab headscarves attend you at your leisure.
Senior crown jewels don't skip at Gillies' balls.
I'm ermine-edged, incarcerated treasure,

fleurs-de-lis, alternate crosses pattée,
costly stones! But Ma'am you'll not forget
how heavy four pounds and twelve ounces weighed,
like promises to north, south, east and west,

nor I your diamond voice as freedom fled,
' . . . I will perform and keep, so help me God'

NICOLETTE GOLDING

LONG LIVE THE QUEEN

Out of Africa a young princess came to be Queen
Something that the world had never seen
No time to grieve, no time to mourn
Destined to be a Queen since the day she was born

Travelling the world widely with Philip by her side
He was so comforting, in him she could confide
They had four children with their troubles too
She sorted out the problems because that what mothers do

Yes, she is our royalty and many are not content
But she has always done her best, but still they won't relent
God bless Her Majesty for the work that she performs
Never mind the doubters, we don't want reforms

In all the years of her reign many changes there has been
The world is now a smaller place and the places that she's seen
Sixty years of pressure, not many would have stood
But the Queen in her majestic way has coped and understood.

BARRY SCOTT CRISP

GOD SAVE THE QUEEN

A beautiful princess, a child of the crown
She stepped in for her father when he was struck down
She carried this country through some troubled times
She has travelled the world and she has done the rounds
Just a young mother and a young wife
To serve her country was a big part of her life
Trained for the job from the day of her birth
To carry this country a part of God's Earth
For the past sixty years she has ruled us all well
She's had her bad times and like us went through Hell
She has lost loved ones just as we do, her children
Have grown and so much have they put her through
Now, sixty years on, we all celebrate for our wonderful Queen
We think she is great, dressed in her splendor
For all to see, as the world watches all now on TV
So let's raise a glass and to her give a cheer
For it's her Diamond Jubilee and the holidays are here
And the next time we sing, 'God Save Our Queen'
Let's thank God every day for her life and what's been

CAROLINE FERGUSON

OUR ELIZABETH

There were those who came before our Elizabeth,
Her namesakes from a different age,
Who forged the kingdom
With a woman's touch of modesty and grace.
So here we are to celebrate our Diamond Queen,
Who has honoured her first vow, to serve her country.
Knowing peace in our time flowered.
Now as with the Coronation
United and without division,
Her reign and country strong,
Pride of Britain in fruition.

MICHELE BEERS

QUEEN'S DIAMOND JUBILEE

Your Royal Highness, Queen Elizabeth the Second
You are the Queen of us all
You are the Queen of Great Britain
People are happy in your reign
May God be with you at all times

You are celebrating 60 years of your services
To your people and to humanity
You are the Queen of love and help
You are the hope of the people in this country
You are celebrating your 60 years of reign

We offer a prayer for you
God bless you our Queen
God help you to reign
For many more years
Longer and longer times

RUHI DARAKSHANI

OUR QUEEN

For sixty years we've seen our Queen
In colours of pink and blue and green.
There is no doubt she is the best,
Always smiles to greet her guests.
Her loyal subjects she smiles and greets,
Her soldiers and horses on the beat.
She smiles and greets them one and all,
Most of her soldiers are quite tall,
I am sure some days she would like to be.
Oh so natural, like you and me,
Her duty first, she does not miss,
But for you and me our days are bliss.
So for today we salute our Queen,
In her colours, pink, blue and green.

ELSIE KEEN

THE KINGDOM IS THE QUEEN

The Kingdom is the Queen,
The Queen this Kingdom.
England referenced itself to her,
Her to this country, her recipient, the heir.
Embracing each other,
Her presence is testimonial,
Such is her influence.
From neophyte to connoisseur,
The nation grew to respect, to admire,
They identified with each others rarity,
Defined each other famously,
Through good times, trying time,
Indifferent times.
We trust in her presence,
In attitudes, in behaviour,
In tradition, in etiquette,
In her consistency,
In her value as saviour.
Enduring with poise and composure,
The Queen prevails, stands firm,
No vagueness, nor hesitancy has blighted
The uncertain extent of her reign.
Her continuum set part the essence of the empire,
She bestowed her vivacity,
Her exuberance, her cheerfulness,

ANDREW JOHN BURNS

THE QUEEN'S DIAMOND JUBILEE

We now rejoice as a nation with pride and high spirit,
As we celebrate Queen Elizabeth II's Diamond Jubilee.
Where you are, young and old, we will join in with glee
To honour our gracious and loving Queen in retreat –
This land we love with hearts open, joyful and clear
Our England, this famous land to us so dear.

Young and old, weak and strong, we will rejoice
And with hands clasped together as we celebrate
Once in a lifetime – June twenty-twelve – the date
Some of us were living at the start, not by choice
For destiny had dictated that the year twenty-twelve
The sixtieth year Her Majesty's reign now delve.

These sixty years will not be forgotten quickly,
For we have enjoyed both good and bad times
Not to compare to present day with cuts and crimes.
We long to return to the good old days, hopefully!
As we pant and look up to our Great Almighty
To herald the twenty-twelve, the Olympic year joyfully.

Hurrah! To our Majesty the Queen and family
We pray for your good health, long life, you will enjoy –
The fruits of your labour whilst your citizens do employ
You extend loving thoughts and gratia to all carefully
Hurrah! To us all surviving the awful days of fury
We pray for our siblings to recover our lost days of glory.

REBECCA ADA WILLIAMS

YOUR FRIENDS IN THE NORTH

Your Majesty's ruled since I was young, a more loyal subject was never among
And when from grace I thought to fall, you stared at me from the classroom wall
And when eating in the ship's mess, you were also there in a shimmering dress
So when the papers print their lies, don't forget that's just to appetise
To slake the thirst of a morbid few, unlike them we think the world of you.

This country, that without the crown, would at first struggle then finally drown
Britannia would sink below the waves and Britons surely then would be slaves
We need a 'firm' hand at the helm, to guide the governance of this realm
We have always had a monarchy, as long as our island's had the sea
So when the fun at you they poke, remember, without you we'd just be a joke.

A lot of people have tried to own, but never achieved the British throne
Only the true may sit in the chair, duty goes with it, at times hard to bear
You must be bred to this estate, of bloodline strong and family great
And when your son succeeds your reign, we know he'll put up with the strain
For when eventually he's allowed, just like you he'll do us proud.

So chin up Ma'am and wear that smile, show them all your regal style
For though the armour may be rusty, of British pride you're still the trustee
Your battle flag still flies aloft, these hearts of oak have not gone soft
And like the guard at 'Dryad' so few, we'd rather like to stick by you.

Respectfully meant this poem's no sham, I remain your obedient servant Ma'am.

ADRIAN G MCROBB

THE QUEEN'S DIAMOND JUBILEE

Come on a journey with me
As we travel through history
Let's take a walk down memory lane
Over the sixty years of the Queen's reign
As we celebrate her Diamond Jubilee

Britain never had it so good
They abolished the ration book
The Queen's Coronation was in fifty-three
People could watch it in front of a TV

Pop music and fashion was the latest craze
It was life in prison for the Krays
Brady and Hindley's murdering days were up
England beat Germany to win the World Cup

Britain was on the decline
Stephen Biko dies in cell (six-one-nine)
Decimals ends a thousand year-old tradition
The IRA attack and bomb Britain

Then came the Falklands War
English clubs were thrown out of European Football
Sutcliffe blames God for his killing spree
The Guildford Four were set free

The poll tax came into play
Britain went into mourning when Princess Di passed away
Police start digging At Fred and Rosemary West's home
The reason why Jill Dando was shot is still unknown

Foot and mouth epidemic hit farmers hard
The Twin Towers fell like a deck of cards
The credit crunch has affected everyone
After a hundred years Woolworth's has gone.

MICHAEL MCNULTY

THE QUEEN, A DIAMOND JUBILEE

'Twas nineteen twenty-six in London
In Bruton Street, by the green,
One April morn
A baby was born
First a princess, then a Queen

Elizabeth Alexandra Mary
A princess she thought she would stay
But a lovesick King changed everything
And the crown was a heartbeat away

In the year nineteen forty-seven
She married her love and her Prince
Beaming with pride
She walked by the side
Of the man who's stayed ever since

I was a cook on the ship Empress of Scotland
When I set my eyes on our Queen
Of course I must stress
She was still our princess
While I was a veg cook and green

On another fine ship called The Gothic
We were waiting in Mombassa Bay
But the Australian tour
Was cancelled – no more
When the King, George the Sixth passed away

The Queen was crowned in Westminster Abbey
Midst surroundings both grand and serene
As the world watched in awe
At the scenes that they saw
A princess grew into a Queen

The union was blessed with four children
In a marriage really divine
Three princes no less
And Anne, a princess
Were born of the union so fine

So in ending this Jubilee story
Let's all speak as one, as a crowd
Saying after sixty great years
Of laughter and tears
Thanks Queen, you're doing us proud

DOUG SHARKEY

PROUD TO BE BRITISH

The 2nd, 3rd, 4th and 5th of June,
From sun till moon,
All this time is to celebrate,
It is going to be so great!
The Queen has reigned for so long,
Not one thing has gone wrong.
She has sat on her throne speaking to the people,
Telling us what was what and what is legal.
Her and her Corgis loved by many,
And her head is on our pennies.
Parties at home or out in the street,
Plenty of new people to meet.
This is our Queen and our country
And she will reign on humbly.
We should be proud, us and the crowd,
Because we are British, we are unique.
As a country,
Wouldn't you agree?

LUCY EDDINGS

Diamond Jubilee

Jubilee, Jubilee,
That's all you're going to hear,
From London to Canada,
Which is many miles from here.

Red, white and blue,
That's what we're going to wear,
Those are the words,
That we need to share.
Mother, wise Queen and so much more.
She does so much for us,
Why can't we do more?

Alice Bannister

Jubilee Bunting

I am a patriot who's true,
Yet at some point and at this time
Of Jubilee much joy,
Red, white and blue
Have saturation point and cloy.
I'm loyal to the last,
But flagging of the three,
Becomes a point past.
And so today, it's green I wear,
Yet to my last my loyalty do swear
And green is true to Queen
And countryside as are the three
I love and bear.
God save our Queen – all colours do declare.

Philip Clements

THE QUEEN'S DIAMOND JUBILEE

I saw the Queen today
I was sitting by the telly,
A million flags were waving
The atmosphere amazing.
People camping out all night,
Just to see a little sight,
Cameras flashing, people singing,
It's our Queen's Diamond Jubilee
That's made history.
The family join her
Side by side
They sing hymns and smile
With great delight.
The Queen puts on a brave face
For the nation.
Her rock, her soulmate
Is not by her side
The Duke is ill
And has watched
Most of the fun from his bed
The Queen carries on
And addresses the nation
Thanking everyone
For the fabulous celebration
Maybe the next one
Will be William and Kate
Announcing a royal baby
Wouldn't that be great?

SHARON LAMBLEY

OUR QUEEN'S DIAMOND JUBILEE

Our Queen's Diamond Jubilee has
Caught the nation's imagination.
Beloved by all her subjects and
Also citizens worldwide, greatly admired
As they are eager to show their demonstrating
Selfless devotion to her
Duty promotion. Not wanting the job at all,
Couldn't let British Constitution stall.
Her father's death came as a shock,
Betimes cruel fate does knock.
There in Kenya, far away, she flew home
Becoming her mother's mainstay.
Becoming only the second monarch to
Reign for sixty years, which brought more
Than its share of tears, as the weight of
The Crown brought her down.
Her son and daughter became divorced,
So to accept it she was forced.
A horrible year she declared and her grief
The nation shared, add to this the death
Of her sister, Margaret, then the passing
Of Princess Diana, and you see into the
Works malign fate had thrown a spanner.
'Black Dog' sat on her shoulders in a
Heavy manner, becoming the dark symbol
On her banner.
Love of horses and her Corgi dogs
Gave her consolation as she
Continued to serve our nation.
Calmly and wisely, she applied herself
With dedication; squaring her shoulders,
Applying them to the wheel, she proved
In her core there was a deal of steel.
Small wonder her subjects did deeply feel
Another weapon in her armoury was
A sense of humour which she privately demonstrated.
Prince Philip spoke his mind,
Often it appeared without thinking.
So the Queen must have had that feeling of sinking.
It was meat and drink to the media
Increasing newspaper sales,
But often arousing criticism by the gales.

He put his foot in his mouth,
But then they would say that
Wouldn't they, just to sell papers and
Make hay. Our Queen rose above all that
Wisely knowing where life was at
And deserves all approbation on her
Diamond Jubilee, with its
River Thames procession finale.

GRAHAM WATKINS

QUEEN ELIZABETH II

We celebrate with our beloved Queen
Her Diamond Jubilee of sixty years
Serving, encouraging and praying
For our nation which she represents
With Prince Philip and the Royal Family
Through the joys and sorrows of life
But always keeping her faith in God
Whose love never changes and
Never fails to provide for all
Who put their trust in His guidance
And bless our homes with joy and peace
Let us follow her example
Share our trust in Jesus with others
And make our homes sanctuaries
Where the next generation can grow up
And use their God-given talents
To make known the love of God
Until God calls them home to His glory
The people sang, 'All people that on Earth do dwell,'
'O praise ye the Lord,'
And 'Guide me O Thou Great Redeemer'
And archbishop Rowan Williams talked about
Finding happiness in seeking the good of others

DAVID COOKE

OPULENCE AND POVERTY

It was a prearranged marriage,
betwixt Opulence and Poverty,
tradition could not be changed,
whereby the rich to the poor were chained.

Never a happy marriage,
but one of convenience.
How else the rich to acquire their wealth,
if not at the expense of Poverty?

The opulence of one,
contrasting the poverty of the other.
No concealing of this fact,
from both the minority and the majority.

Hence, the waving, cheering crowds attending the ceremony,
all knew of their respective places in society.
Opulence, relied upon Poverty to sustain the life style of their families whilst Poverty was
dependent on their favours.

Food and wealth a'plenty, no worries at all,
Opulence – always in splendour, at all banquets and fine balls.
Whilst Poverty toiled, scraped away, each working day,
in fear of redundancy, increased prices, of which they had no say!

And yet, Poverty waved their flags and rejoiced,
when Opulence indicated all so to do.
For such is the power and wealth,
of The Establishment,
albeit in-numbers, just a comparative few!

PETER MAHONEY

TROUBLE ON THE JUBILEE LINE

I unpacked my patriotism and laid it starkly on the bed,
I left it there to air, to clear the mildew of unuse and just to let others know it existed.
Maybe the stale emissions, the moulded contours might recall the boy gone by?
The boy once pictured in the paper, anoraked by electric-blue cagoule,
NHS bespectacled and plaster eye-patched, I can still feel who he was -
A smiling spade breaking soil to make a sapling offer for the Jubilee,
Paisley shirted and heavy collared at the neck.
Collared it seems to me now, as much by enforced duty as the large patterned wings
of fabric.

I unravelled my patriotism, the edge of which cuts at my fingers and my conscience,
Its serrated outline now snagged-jagged by the moths of time, catches like hangnails, as I
unfold its faded crosses.
And in unfurled creases and crevices, bold painted lines have cracked
and turned to dust.
In flapping out the flag the grists of grief have split from the childish chaff of ignorance,
Wry recognition that schoolboy shoes could with one mud-shod slip
have denied that sycophantic plant,
Have cut the root from branch and in some small way pre-empted
the foolish sense of honour at the task.

I'll bury my patriotism under some bleak cement, the rejection of parasitic regality.
But to give it due place, the crass, en-mass have subsumed it
into their profanity and anger.
Expletive in its enmity of single fingered salutes to foreign foes on fields of sport,
To the unknowing blinds still craven loyalty the boy in the paper has long been lost,
The grass and garden, the soiled memory of the act, indeed, is now
A tarmac parking space, lifeless, grey and flat.
And the confined roots, the last confines of that once patriotic tree, are wrapped
in my contempt.

The tree is dead and I will not mourn it.

NEIL BENTON

THE QUEEN'S DIAMOND JUBILEE

The Thames winds a path through London
The crowds are amass on each side
Waiting for the Queen with anticipation
Their hearts are bursting with pride
This lady, although short in stature
Had a heart that's been torn wide apart
With the crown came the loss of her father
This of course was only the start.
As she sat on her barge, decked in flowers
Perhaps she thought back over the years
Unlike her father she knew her destiny
Willingly embracing the flags and the cheers
She points and says to Philip
'Oh look, there's that daughter of mine
Dressed up in her smart uniform
She really looks quite fine.
Look, also our son Andrew
His girls are enjoying this day
Oh Heavens! There's the War Horse'
She laughs as it trotted away.
She wished her mummy had been here
To see this cleverly made, rearing horse
She always really loved her animals
A love she inherited of course.
'Oh Philip she cried, 'Those tiny ships
Think of all that they have done
And all those men rowing hard
They look like they're having fun.'
Looking further down the barge
She spots two very handsome lads
She's so proud of these two grandsons
Overcoming the loss they had,
Pulling her shawl so much tighter
For the weather has turned quite cold
'I wish I had worn a warmer coat
I keep forgetting that I am getting old.'
'My dear you look so beautiful
Not everyone can wear white.'
'You're talking rubbish Philip
But then you might be right.'
Together they watch London Bridge
Its jaws are opening wide

As slowly they chug there under
And out the other side.
She looks around in wonder
Such fantastic things she's seen
Everyone has worked so hard
What a marvellous day it's been.
'Although my legs are aching
From standing all the way
I wish that I could thank them all
For this utterly glorious day.'
When the Jubilee barge is docked
Allowing the Queen at last to depart
She looks around for a mug of tea
To warm the cockles of her heart.

PAMELA LAFLIN

THE QUEEN TO ME . . .

This is to celebrate the Queen's Diamond Jubilee,
Some people may celebrate it more than me.
The one thing she does on her victories is to share,
That's one of the reasons why I care.

We see the Queen as an inspiration,
That's why we show our dedication.
But one of the things that means something to me,
Is to show my congrats on her Jubilee.

But I don't just see her as a Queen,
Someone that you haven't really seen.
A mother of four
And a grandma of more
And not just a crown that's she wore.

Sixty years of being our Queen,
I can honestly say she's the best I've seen!

MELISHA BASRA

ELIZABETH OUR QUEEN

The Queen does reign in majesty,
She wears the crown with dignity;
Of noble birth and pedigree,
She reigns in peace o'er land and sea.

With family, her source of pride,
And loyal consort by her side,
With corgis lying at her feet,
The royal picture is complete.

As head of State and Monarchy
She plays her roles with dignity,
From playing host to diplomats
To meetings with state bureaucrats.

On the world's stage she plays her parts,
Uniting minds and blending hearts;
Her work for charities abound,
Bringing good cheer to all around.

Sixty long years since she was crowned,
Her reign throughout the world renowned;
Let tributes flow o'er land and sea,
In this her Diamond Jubilee.

Let beacons shine and church bells ring,
Let concert bands and choirs sing,
Let infant voices, full of glee,
Proclaim the Royal Jubilee.

DAVID LOUGHER

THE QUEEN'S DIAMOND JUBILEE

There was this day, one special day,
that will only happen once,
this day was the month after May;
it was the Diamond Jubilee dance.

This day is where we celebrate,
The Queen's Jubilee,
We feel this is the great,
The greatness of our dreams.

We celebrate the British pride,
of the Queen and country,
as we are full of might,
putting all our love out for she.

The Queen, the one and only,
the one and only Queen,
she never makes us feel lonely and her kindness can be seen.

Flags waving all around,
as people cheer and shout,
the longest living monarch ever we have found,
anyone living would be proud.

Chug, chug, chug, as the boat went along,
looking around with a smile on her face,
passing people singing the British sing song,
waving perfectly with elegant grace.

Your Majesty the Queen,
on this very special day,
everyone around her
are going 'Hip hip hooray!'

SAMUEL HARRISON

O Regina, Queen Elizabeth II Of England Born 1926

The Queen's royal barge,
Upon the mighty Thames,
With regal, glorious splendour,
Sixty years, Her Majesty's golden rule.

O fair bright monarch and Queen,
Good Queen of England,
Divinely ordained by God,
Thy sovereign of the world.

Supreme and victorious,
With probity and immaculate manners,
Decked in fabulous jewels,
Diamonds, rubies and sapphires.
Your Diamond Jubilee,
Happy, bright and gay,
Graceful and virtuous,
Ruling with authority and power.

O beloved Queen, immortal forever,
Lovelier with age, O Regina,
Queen Elizabeth II of England,
O London and Buckingham Palace.

Where the Household Cavalry ride,
With silver breastplates,
Triumphant in your finest hour,
With glory and bouquets of flowers.

O God save our dutiful Queen,
With modesty while praising
All of her majestic achievements.
Down through the years.

Well loved by the British nation,
With kings, queens, princes and lords,
In 1953 your golden coronation,
O Lord protect our gracious Queen.

James Stephen Cameron

MOTHER TO BRITAIN

To our glorious Queen, Elizabeth the Second
A simple list of the things that you have done for us;
You have been by our side in spirit and mind,
You have been so caring and loving for your people,
You have been out through the utmost heartache,
You have been able to experience the greatest joy,
For sixty years you have reigned in Great Britain,
You have been loved, praised and honoured for those sixty years,
You have been a mother to Britain for sixty years,
A mother we will cherish and want to keep,
We all have two mothers; our birth mother
And you, our Mother of Britain.

NYISHA REBEKAH COLQUHOUN

BRITISH QUEEN OF THE CHAIR

Now this the story, all about how
The Queen of England just got crowned.
And I'd like to take a minute, just sit right there,
I'll tell you how I became the Queen upon this chair.

Near Westminster Abbey born and raised,
In the palace is where I spent most of my days.
Chilling out, maxing, hunting all day,
Playing some polo, all happy and gay.
When my great daddy died, that was no good,
But I became the Queen of my neighbourhood.
I dated the Duke and we got wed,
And gave birth to Charles, Andrew, Anne and Ed.

I curtseyed for the crown and when it came near,
Jewels glistened and the crowd all cheered.
If anything, I could say that this crown is rare,
But I thought, *forget it, this home is my chair!*

I pulled up to the palace about seven or eight
And I yelled to the driver, 'Yo Jones, knight you later.'
Looked at the United Kingdom, I was finally there,
To sit on my throne as the Queen of the chair.

REBECCA HODDS, CAYLEIGH HARDWICK, HAYLEY STEWART & LEAH MURDEN

ROYALTY'S GOT TALENT

Charles is forecasting the weather for the Royal event today,
He laughs and says, 'It's a good job it's not a bloody Bank Holiday.'
The Royals are presenting their own show in aid if the Jubilee,
But some events are not going completely successfully.

The Duchess of York has gone missing and is nowhere to be found,
She was put in charge of Ticket sales but has since gone underground.
Andrew's coughed up all the cash for the money that's been used,
The Queen has made a statement saying, 'We are not amused.'

The horses' hay has all been chomped; the show is set to play,
But there's no horse to romp around, it's Zara all the way.
Mike has had a bit to drink and shed his shirt and jeans,
He's asking Countess Sophie if she'll play at kings and queens.

The Queen has trained her Corgi dogs to give a dog display,
But soon the dogs get bored and then all start to run astray.
Philip's rigged a tent up, with the words in big, bold lights,
'Queue up here to get your treatment for those Corgi bites.'

The Queen is first on stage to start performing karaoke,
Beginning with a Queenie version of the Hokey Cokey.'
'One puts one's left arm in and then one's left arm out,
Then one does the Hokey Cokey and then shakes one's crown about.'

Everyone has looked to see how Will and Kate arrive,
They've dropped right in from up above by doing a sky dive.
They land upon the catwalk to head up the fashion show,
With Beatrice and Eugenie doing fashion shoots below.

Will is making eyes at Kate, he's clearly in the mood,
But Kate has had enough and says, 'I'll do it like a dude.'
She boots him off the catwalk with a very nifty kick,
Singing, 'Do it like a mandem if your guy acts like a dick.'

Her Majesty scoots over to the catwalk, double speed,
'Kate darling, I have just the very thing I know you need.
A quiet little holiday for you in my nice tower,
It gives one greatest pleasure to be using one's Girl Power!'

Her Majesty is pleased at her most witty little take
And then the Princess Royal comes over carrying a cake.
It's coloured like the Union Jack, on top there is a throne,
God Save the Queen is playing now on everybody's phone.

Everyone now gathers round and starts to sing along,
With words quite unfamiliar to the public for this song.

'God save the monarchy
Give work to royalty
We're really keen
We'll open fetes for you
Christen a boat or two
Turn up for any do
God Save the Queen.'

YVONNE NOWAKOWSKI

THE QUEEN'S DIAMOND JUBILEE

60 years on the throne,
Our Queen Elizabeth has called her home,
Buckingham Palace in London, Windsor Castle too,
Sandringham House in Norfolk to name just a few.

Tourists come to see her and the changing of the guard,
Marching up and down all day, must be very hard,
She'll send you to the Tower, if you give her any cheek
And 'off with your head,' she'll say, it won't be very sweet.

Our Queen is oh so regal
In her lovely royal gown,
You might find her at Ascot
But not at Epsom Down.

With a royal wave and regal glance she walks about the street,
Her people waiting patiently to shake her hand and greet,
You need to mind your Ps and Qs when speaking with the Queen
And raise your glass to make a toast, to the best that's ever been.

It's best if you just celebrate her 60 years of reign,
'Cause this is a one-time offer that she won't repeat again,
Street parties all around the towns,
Flags, balloons, cakes and gowns,
Children playing tag and games,
Parents calling out their names,
They'll have such fun in the streets today,
In the most quintessential way.

RICHARD MANTLE, ASHLEY LETCH, MICHAEL BARRELL, BERNADETTE SCRAFTON,
IAN BANNISTER, GREGORY DURHAM & MICHAEL SUTTON

ELIZABETH R 1952 – THE PROMISE

Teacups were chinking
Glasses were tinkling
Laughter filled the air,
Trestle tables were laid
With cakes – homemade
Celebrations everywhere.

Princess to be Queen
What a glorious scene
Golden carriage went passing by,
Loud shouts of 'Hooray!'
Truly historic day
Flags were flying high.

Once again tables are laid
With cream scones – homemade
Amid streamers, red, white and blue
Diamond Jubilee Queen
Britain and Commonwealth have seen
'I GIVE MY LIFE TO SERVING YOU –'

Elizabeth R 2012 – The Promise
Fulfilled . . .

JEAN MACKENZIE

JUBILEE

Day she gets crowned, you hardly see a thing,
at worship round that eight-inch goggle box,
Rosearean Club, with half the parish wrapt,
like a sympathetic string. As rare back there
as outhouse loos today and rationed, wireless
king, ghosts float before your eyes, reflect
grey-flannel world outside. Mind set one mean
street, ranger ride away, sneak home to build
an outlaw roost behind the chicken coop.
You're down four feet before you know, see off
light rain with hessian and cane, off-cut
broadloom for floor, snug as a grave. You swot
star-spangled comic book, Jumping-Jack-Flash
in mask, republican, suck sweets and dream.

PETER BRANSON

A JUBILEE OCCASION

Jubilee, Jubilee, Jubilee, it's all we seem to hear,
Jubilee, Jubilee, Jubilee, it sure is drawing near,
Most will enjoy the celebrations and have the best time ever
And we will get a day off work, now that is very clever.
West Hoathly will pull all the stops for this momentous event,
They'll have a Diamond Jubilee supper in a gigantic tent.
A Royal Scarecrow competition, to add a little fun
And a very nice prize for the winner to be won.
A pageant of floats going through the streets
And vendors selling all sorts of memorable treats.
The children will dress up in a Jubilee theme
And some stalls may sell refreshments and even ice cream.
A souvenir programme to commemorate
And a tug-of-war, so don't you dare be late.
On Sunday we'll have a picnic on the village green
And a prize for the best scarecrow that they have ever seen.
The children will dress up in a royal theme
And I bet there'll be quite a few dressed as the Queen,
The marquee will present a blues band,
So all in all it will be quite grand.
Another band for the picnic, jazz this time around
And we can all have a boogie there upon the ground.
The lighting of the beacon will be on the menu
And a firework display will end the venue.
A drink in the Vinols or the Cat
With a hip hip hooray, that's the end of that.

SUSAN JOHNSTONE

QUEEN'S JUBILEE

On this special occasion
May we celebrate the special event,
May our Queen remember
This special day
And hope our Queen
Will have good health,
God Save the Queen.

D HALLFORD

A FAIRYTALE DAY

It was a wonderful day to be a child living in London!
Waving a flag as the Coronation Coach rolled by.
Heavy rain poured down but we felt no need of the sun,
Queen Elizabeth II, newly crowned queen, lit up our sky.
It was a fairytale day, one remembered for a lifetime!
Silvery white horses pulled her coach of scarlet and gold,
As a child, only six, it was a magical scene sublime,
It was like fairytales, about princesses of old.

We left The Mall, travelled by tube train and trolley,
To join relatives living near Willesden's Jubilee clock.
On arrival I was given a Coronation peg-dolly,
At Aunt Else's house I dressed in my party frock.

When, by afternoon, it stopped raining, the magic was set to continue,
Men put up trestle tables and seats for a party in the street!
Aunt Else covered the tables with crepe paper of red, white and blue.
I helped fill tables till they creaked under the weight of good things to eat.

For children born to post-war rationing, such a spread was like a dream,
Ham sandwiches, pork pies, sausage rolls; the finest feast we'd ever seen!
Then, red, green and orange jelly, with blancmange and mock cream.
Before eating a toast was raised and we sang, 'God Save our Queen'

Entertainment followed, guest's party pieces were perfect for that,
My cousin, Ethel, proved herself to be a tap dancing star,
Carrying red, white and blue ribbons, doves flew from a magician's hat.
Then finally, came two clowns, who drove around in their collapsing car.

At dusk coloured lights illuminated Queen Victoria's Jubilee clock in style,
We took a stroll around the streets until it grew properly dark.
We walked a few yards to Willesden Junction, watched trains for a while,
Then to my surprise, at that hour of night, turned into the park.

Dad swung me up on his shoulders; what is this game?
A loudspeaker blared; 'We hope you enjoy our fantastic firework show.'
On a wall appeared, 'God Bless Queen Elizabeth II,' spelt in silvery flame.
Rockets soared up, their red, white and blue sparks set the sky aglow.

A blinding flash preceded a deafening bang, crashing and whistling,
Screams followed the explosion, when sparks started raining down.
'Wow! That was a good-un,' said Uncle Sid, 'Really made your ears sing.
Bet they can't keep it up! It's cost more than her diamond crown.'
The loudspeaker crackled, 'Sorry for the early end to our display,
They all fired at once.' 'Well, at least it went with a bang!' called Uncle Sid.
The loudspeaker continued, 'We only hope it didn't spoil your day.'
Later, at home, Aunt Else said, 'They must have forgotten to close the lid.'

JULIE FREEBORN

JUBILATIONS DIAMOND STYLE

They are celebrating in the streets,
There's merriment and cheer,
Three score years Her Majesty completes
This Diamond Jubilee year.

There are flags being hoisted in the air,
Banners being waved about,
Queen Elizabeth II this Jubilee year
Is sixty years not out.

The longest reign since Queen Victoria,
Much mourned in 1901,
Queen Elizabeth II they're cheering for her,
Now her Diamond year has come.

They are celebrating in the towns,
There's parties being held for sure,
Three score years this Queen of ours
And here's to many more.

Equalling the reign of King George III, 1760 to 1820,
There's many a cheer this diamond year
And many a glass being emptied.

They are celebrating nationwide
Now that the time is here.
To Her Majesty with the greatest of pride,
This Diamond Jubilee year.

PETER TERENCE RIDGWAY

DIAMOND DAY

There is a special day in British hearts
A Diamond Day, it's true
The best British party ever
We are the guests, me and you
At the heart of it is someone special
Our Queen . . . she is always there
To lend support to our nation
I guess that is why we all care.
Queen Elizabeth, an unforgettable woman
For sixty years she has served us all
Representing Britain for us
And she is the best of them all.
So that is why we come together
On her very special day
Forgetting all worries and troubles
To celebrate her Diamond Jubilee Day.

JOYCE HUDSPITH

MAD MONARCHY

She's a greedy gluttonous despot
The Queen of leeches
Is a farce of a civil list
That exists for the past

Roll on the president of the republic
So the public may have
Proper democratic representation.

The British Isles is a partitioned realm of confusion
She reigns with a sceptre of sectarianism
The Commonwealth empire is the Union Jack
Dripping with blood
From the wars of the succession.

MATTHEW LEE

DIAMOND JUBILEE CELEBRATION

How many
Is that?
Is there any
Union Jack
Bunting,
Party equipment
And a hat
(Union Jack
Coloured)?
Any excuse
To let
A/the
Celebration
Loose.

How could we
Forget?
And reminded
As a regular
Event are
Better at
Remembering
How to do
It.
As if familiar
Routine
Rhymed
With long
Reigning Queen.

NICOLA BARNES

BRITAIN'S QUEEN LIZ

For six decades we have seen
Very many varies, pretty hats
Of Her Majesty
And seen very many long red mats

We must feel pride inside
When many beautiful outfits we have seen
Always with a smile to match
Travels Her Majesty our Queen

But is there another side
Beyond the pomp and ceremony
To this our Queen Liz
Wife, mother and lover of her Corgi

Immaculately dressed
As she travels town after large town
Despite her many hats
I feel her favourite is her crown

Taking her father's place there
Into a vast kingdom she did delve
Six decades to show
In this Jubilee twenty-twelve
Congratulations!

BARBARA SHERLOW

A ROYAL LANDMARK DAY

Spending the day at the nursery with the children I hold so dear,
Celebrating the Queen's special Diamond Jubilee year.
Dressed as a princes, princesses, kings and queens,
Making the occasion a very patriotic scene.
Celebrating Her Majesty and everything royal today,
Or remembering watching the Coronation, on that very special day.
Great Britain blessed to still have a monarchy,
Beholding the rare and true Crown Jewel of our country.
A queen for sixty years or a fairytale one for a day,
We'll be joining the nation,
Celebrating Your Majesty's achievement
In a very landmark way.

EMMA LOUISE GARDNER

ALL MY CHILDREN

All my children sit together now
And share a common purpose,
All my children stand together now
And speak with a common tongue.

All my children came to me alone
Each one with their own ideals,
And all my children fought on and on
Each believing they were right.

All my children caused heart-felt grief
As they destroyed all for nothing.
All my children wounded me deeply
As they turned against themselves.

But now they are all in my embrace,
As they come to me together.
All my children hold hands as one
To salute me, their parent, their friend, their Queen.

SUE GERRARD

LET THEM EAT CAKE

Your Majesty, Your Grace, my Lords, Ladies and Gentlemen
Due to unprecedented and calamitous circumstances
Tonight's celebratory banquet is cancelled
No the chef de cuisine is not indisposed
Nor the menu impaired
Neither are there any amenities lacking

No, this outrageous consequence results from another source
A fountainhead of frightening potential
Which if left unaddressed
Could ripen fast for sinister replication
– The kitchen hands and dishwashers are on strike
– With all waiters showing solidarity
Is it possible they have reasoned through our dependency
For the necessity of the status quo to be maintained?

Your Majesty, Your Grace
My Lord, Ladies and Gentlemen – if this be so
Then may the mercy of God be upon us.

KEVIN COBLEY

OUR BELOVED QUEEN

When I was a child I would dream
Of being a queen.
But knowing now how much she works,
Travelling miles and shaking hands,
She never shirks,
I am glad that I am not.
We are truly blessed
In having our Queen,
So like her mother she has been,
Both did and she still does
So much for the realm.
We do not realise the strain,
Maybe at her age, there may be pain,
We, her people, do not know
Things she feels and does not show.
Her prince has had his price to be paid,
For together they are as one,
Together so much work has been done.
Yes, we her people are truly blessed.
Long may she continue to reign,
Without our Queen
Life would never be the same.

GRACE MAYCOCK

DIAMOND DAYS

A nation proud and steeped in history,
Held in awe by the world for its honesty
And the birth of sensible nobility,
As it beholds the Queen's Diamond Jubilee.

Our monarch rules our hearts and country,
With honour, trust and bravery,
A realm ruled just with majesty,
Britain safe under Queen Elizabeth's sovereignty.

KIERAN DAVIS

QUEEN ELIZABETH II

Post-war Britain
And there she was –
A young wife and mother –
And then a newly Royal Queen –
Both loyal and dedicated
Her work to begin
To lead her people
Into an unforgettable era
Of change and through wars,
Economic fluctuations
And technical advances
And yet she remained
Steadfast and patient,
Setting a fine example
For all subjects to follow –
A truly majestic woman
Who reigned sixty years
With flawless devotion
To a Commonwealth she loves.

DIANA KWIATKOWSKI RUBIN

DIAMOND JUBILEE

We who love you beyond compare
This glorious day with you we share
We, your loyal subjects, are mighty proud
With our hearts and souls forever bound
To you, our most precious, constant Queen
A heartfelt bondage pure and clean

Around the world all hearts rejoice
Proclaiming with a clear, loud voice
A happiness, immense, serene
A Diamond Jubilee for our cherished Queen
Eternal bondage forever lies
Diamond years, unbroken ties

SHULA BAILEY

JEWEL IN THE CROWN

A sparkling diamond is our Queen
60 years, much changes seen
Early June – toast her good health
Both home and in the Commonwealth.

When she ascended to the throne
Treetops – Kenya – thoughts alone
Elizabeth R – pale morning light
Sad Norfolk tidings overnight.

Throughout her reign she's been our rock,
Hectic mileage round the clock
Up and down Great Britain's length
At 85 an inner strength.

This special lady we adore
Flags and bunting by the score
Come celebrate in verse with me
Her historic Jubilee.

STEVE GLASON

WHAT CAN ONE SAY ABOUT THE JUBILEE

Not Much,
A woman born with a golden spoon
Not silver.
For all her life she knew no worries
Only enjoyment,
Oh! such choices to make in life
Pearls or rubies?
Her servants are the ones to praise
Hard workers,
They are the diamonds in
This Jubilee.

ELIZABETH MURRAY-SHIPLEY

HER MAJESTY THE QUEEN – THE DIAMOND JUBILEE 1952-2012

Her Majesty the Queen
She is wonderful and bright
What a pleasant Queen we have

A special day awaits her
The Diamond Jubilee has arrived
It is sixty years today

She has been on the throne
For a long time
She is still wonderful and well

We will show our support
And we will think of her
We will bow to her

We will feel proud
And we will produce a toast
To Her Majesty the Queen

Thank you so much
For your hard work for Great Britain
The great tours around the country
And for supporting us

Let the bells ring
Let the flags out

She will remain in the hearts
Of the British people

TOM BREALEY

THE QUEEN –WHY SHE'S THE BEST

Elizabeth II is a Jubilee Queen
Who though now an 'oldie'
Is not a 'has been'
She's worked hard for us
Throughout her long reign
And although she's 'glorious'
She is never vain!

She's seen us through bad times
It can't have been fun
To be both a queen and a wife and a mum
To have to wear crowns when your feet need a soak
To record all the soaps so you can go plant an oak!

She has though kept smiling and waving us on
Through many strikes and power cuts
Spring wet, summer short and winter long
But even when the days won't end
We know she's there – one constant friend

She is descended from a very long line
Of kings, queens and conquerors
All perfectly fine But some of their histories
Quite clearly state
That though they were many
They often weren't great!

Take William the Conqueror, sometimes called Bill
He shot Harold down as he stood on a hill
He looked at the sky cos he thought it might rain
Got a shaft in the eye and did not reign again

Or Charles II, quite different from Dad
Not proud and haughty but a bit of a lad
The plague and the fire nearly laid London flat
I am sure the next Charles will do better than that!

Then came Queen Anne, does anyone care?
She left lots of house to prove she was there
It seems a bit hard that all that is said
When her name is mentioned is Anne, 'Oh, she's dead'

Epilogue
Each age has it virtues and each has its pains
The people will grumble whoever may reign
But today we are lucky and you'll know what I mean
When I ask you to say with me, God save our Queen!

ANDREA PAYNE (MARSTON)

A JUBILEE CELEBRATION – HER GRACIOUS MAJESTY QUEEN ELIZABETH II

All Hail! All Power! All Glory!
Sixty years to tell the story,
The saga that has stood the test of time
And spread the message through every clime.

Let the trumpets sound loud and clear,
Let all music be pleasant to the ear,
Let the golden sun shine more brightly,
Giving thanks to the Almighty.

Let the balmy breeze with scented air
Encircle the world from flowers rare,
Let the mighty rivers caress the banks,
Giving the Lord special thanks.

Let the moon mysterious and benign
Over her dominions gently shine,
Let the stars twinkle with delight,
Illuminating the heavens with silver light.

Let the people rise and sing,
Let the church bells proudly ring,
Let the good news spread far and wide,
Let love, joy and peace abide.

Let the gentle rain from Heaven above
Tell Her Majesty of our constant love,
Sixty glorious years of dedication,
Accept our thanks from a grateful nation.

IRENE GREENALL

HER MAJESTY ELIZABETH II – A TRIBUTE

She was born Elizabeth Alexandra Mary Windsor in 1926,
No one imagined she would be Queen,
Her uncle, Edward VIII, abdicated for love,
He created the greatest royal scandal ever seen.

Heir apparent at the tender age of eleven,
Groomed to inherit her future role on the throne,
Exiled temporarily to Windsor Castle during the war years,
To a victorious nation and London she returned home.

In Prince Philip she found her consort and soulmate,
At the Royal Naval College, Dartmouth, they met when she was thirteen,
Sub Lieutenant Philip Mountbatten stood out from the crowd,
He was tall, handsome and eighteen.

With marriage and motherhood, Princess Elizabeth blossomed,
Until fate intervened in 1952,
Her beloved father, King George VI died,
Now her responsibilities grew.

In 1953, Her Majesty, Elizabeth II was crowned,
Everyone rejoiced at her Coronation,
A changing Britain emerged over the next twenty-five years,
With the Silver Jubilee we were euphoric with celebration.

Her Majesty's world though slowly crumbled,
Her children divorced and Windsor Castle was burnt down,
The death of Princess Diana brought the nation to a standstill,
What future was there now for the crown?
Slowly Her Majesty rebuilt the Royal Family,
They became closer to the public they served.
She guided and cared for a new generation of Royals,
Her Golden Jubilee brought adulation and respect well deserved.

It's 2012 and the Diamond Jubilee,
We wait to celebrate 60 years of her reign,
She is a phenomenon like Queen Victoria,
Without her will the House of Windsor be the same?

FINE BULICIRI

THE GENERATION THAT REMEMBERED
(FOR MY GRANDPARENTS)

There is no easy way for me to explain
What this one woman means to myself.
How she watched those defend and die for her reign
With the dignity laid bare for those about.

The modern day man of our once humble nation
Says her power in Great Britain has gone
That she now goes on by, just through the motion
Of a monarch no longer in the sun

Alas these people that speak, yet much less think
Are the people who get given attention
Those that keep important virtues on the brink
Are the voices that we hear less often

My parents' parents are the ones who knew best
This lady in glory, that gave over her life
To the good of the good, mother to the rest
No pride and no fall, a smile during strife

She would sit at dinners, smiling politely
She would stand and applaud when needed
She would speak to crowds on foreign soil wisely
She would listen yet never be cheated

Values in faith and a faith in her people
Conveyed the love that was so modestly given
Making even the poorest of all feel regal
And the lazy? Optimistically driven

'Fantastic she is,' was a grandparents phrase
'How on Earth does she keep going?'
'Gets no recognition you know, giving up her days'
'But she does it for us, the unknowing'

Just some of the quotes from the people who cared
For this woman was theirs to be heard and seen
There from the start, the one that they served
Was the girl they grew up with, their Queen

ROBERT KINNEAR

A CUPCAKE FOR THE QUEEN

'Please, no royal banquet!
Forget the fancy spread!
Cake,' declared Her Majesty
'Is all I want instead.'

'This Jubilee is hungry work
One 'aint getting any thinner!
So cake will reign on my parade
And I will choose the winner.'

So bakeries throughout the land
Began to beat and mix,
In a national competition
To give the Queen her fix.

Double chocolate fondue creams,
Victoria surprises,
Lemon drizzles, toffee swizzles,
Cakes of all disguises.

Cakes the size of palaces,
Cakes made into gowns,
Cakes with frills, designed to thrill
Like royal wedding gowns.

The famous streets of London
Were paved with cake and cream,
For the Diamond Queen of England
It was quite the sweetest scene.

She nibbled through the palace gates,
Down The Mall she munched,
After tasting all Trafalgar scoffed,
'One really must skip lunch.'

But on she gobbled gallantly,
Until finally she found
A cake, not grand, nor fancy,
But of which England could be proud.

It was thrust before Her Majesty
Right outside St Paul's
And little did its baker know
It met with such applause.

'I made a baker's dozen,'
Said the little girl distressed,
'But I've only got this one left now
And it's really not my best.'

'Daddy ate my favourite one,
My brothers stole two more,
My granny had her fiends to tea,
So she asked me for four.

I caught the bus to London
But I forgot to bring my purse,
So I sold one to the driver,
And a kindly looking nurse.'

'But that leaves two more cupcakes,'
Said Her Majesty, now keen,
To learn who deserved the royal cakes
More than the loyal Queen.

'Well sadly Ma'am, a passing horse
Took one for his tea,
So that leaves just this one now,
Will you share it with me?'

Said Queen, 'In sixty years upon the throne,
I've shared a lot of cake,
'Tis not the recipes I recall
But all the friends I make.'

And so the winning baker
Held her crowned cupcake aloft,
A symbol of new friendship
For her grateful Queen to scoff.

CLAIRE PRICE

THE QUEEN'S DR MARTIN'S JUBILANT DIAMOND BOX

When they come down the Thames
The river and city will stop
60 silver rivers
Queen Elizabeth the Second
The Duke of Edinburgh
I painted a Dr Martin's boot box I found in a bin
On the Hammersmith and City Line Platform
In Ladbroke Grove
I sketched in Queen in biro and ink
Also Prince Philip inside and outside
As I rode on the train.
When I got down to crisis
I gave it the works
Screen printed with colours
Silver and gold and made up the diamonds myself
The barge they will come on
The Thames and he City
The original box may now be a jewel of its own
Since nineteen-sixty
Could it be Prince Philip who abandoned the box?
Would he be making a connection
With the first original Dr Martin's 1960 boot?

Not sure if they wear lace-up Dr Martin's
The Queen and Prince Philip are lovers of art
I'm waiting to cheer them with joy
And look out for the prints of their soles
And crown them a frame in my box.

JOHN JOSEPH SHEEHY

THE DIAMOND JUBILEE

Sixty years upon the throne
Has sat the Queen we call our own
Sharing all our hopes and fears
Our laughter, joy and even tears.

Governments have come and gone
But our lives can carry on
Because we know Her Majesty
Will always bring stability

All the emotions we go through
We know that you have felt them too
Because for all the public parts we see
You're only human, just like me

Your Majesty, this year we honour you
Your reign, your rule, your service too
And wish you happiness and health
Throughout Britain and the Commonwealth

So with common voice let's give a cheer
That people all around the world can hear
Not once, not twice, but again and again
God save the Queen, long may she reign

OLIVIA POLLARD

QUEEN

I am but flesh
Yet I hold the weight
Of a crown, sceptre
Orb and throne.
Hold up an edifice,
Complex as an
Astronomer's view
Through a telescope
Fixed on the
Margins of the
Solar system.
Yet I am
But flesh
Stretched
On a tapestry
Woven back
Through space and time
My signature
Caught up
In a web
Of names
Associations
Entangling me
In obligations
I must fulfil
To keep my head
Above water
My feet on
Land.
Towards unity
Of pride
Ritual
Symbolic
Flourish
Where I wave
My one hand
That is
But flesh
Amid all
Which will
Outlive me.

If I keep
Afloat
Pass
The baton
On.

GILLIAN SUMMERSON

THE QUEEN'S DIAMOND JUBILEE 1952 -2012

Heavy the burden 1952,
Heartbroken, loss of the King.
New married life, new responsibilities.
Head of the Church, just one.

Trials abound in any situations,
State, Church and family.
Loss of dear ones burdens the way.
Shouldering of tasks is great.

Close family trials,
Head of State challenges,
Leader of Faith, all so important,
All borne with dignity and pride.

Yes! From early demands in the fifties,
Throughout the ensuing decades,
Our Queen, Elizabeth the Second,
Has stood firm with Prince Philip, His Grace.

A country needs guidance,
An example of love and faith.
The Queen has given both.
God Bless, from all her subjects.

RALPH WATKINS

An Ode To Her Majesty

Put our your flags and buntings
For the time is getting near
A Royal Celebration
The Queen's 60th year.

The beacons will be lit
At night throughout the land
With all the pomp and ceremony
And maybe even a brass band.

We're celebrating the Jubilee
And doing it in style
With fireworks and festivities
We're going that extra mile.

So raise your glass and toast
A celebratory cheer
As we wish Her Majesty
A Happy Diamond Year.

Jayne Vogan

Ode To The Queen

And sixty years she's bore the Crown
Duty bound on prudent throne
A life that's open throughout the years
Love and laughter plus sighs and tears.

And so her love still by her side
Touching fingertips to gently guide
In private times they collect their thoughts
Ready for when she next holds court.

And still she smiles and waves to greet
The powerful with Corgis at her feet
Discretion and patience, integrity go,
A sea of knowledge that will softly flow

And days in tiaras with diamonds bright
The next horse riding with pure delight
The Queen's zest for life shines through
While we, the public sing, 'God Bless You.'

Linda Hurdwell

GLORIOUS 60

The year 2012 is upon us all,
It has been ten long years since
We celebrated your Golden Jubilee.
The nation still looks up to you
As Queen, as Sovereign and our beloved Head of State.

You have now reigned for six long decades,
Upon your Royal throne,
Through good times and bad times
Happy times and sad times.

Standing before you was a dashing young man,
In his Naval uniform, his name was Philip Mountbatten,
Whom you were soon to marry and he would become the
Duke of Edinburgh and become the longest
Running consort.

The Windsors have grown in number
With your sons and daughter alike.
Prince Charles, Princess Anne, Prince Andrew and
Prince Edward, are all your cherished children.

You have many grandchildren,
Some of whom have grown up
And flown the nest.
They love you all the same.
Those precious memories still remain.

In April 2011
Prince William married his beloved bride
Kate Middleton.
Which was celebrated in front of the world
In a big, fairytale wedding which will be remembered for years to come.

Also in July 2011 Zara Philips married
Mike Tindall, a famous rugby player
In Scotland on a lovely summer's day.
It was not a big, fairytale wedding,
But a much more private affair.

The crowds are standing before you
To celebrate your Diamond Jubilee.
As you stand upon the balcony of the Palace
Looking down on your proud nation,
May you long reign over us.
God save the Queen.

RACHEL BROTHERTON

THANK YOU YOUR MAJESTY

From Princess to Monarch
Mother and Queen
Sixty long years, what changes we've seen
You have shared your life with us
Some happy, some sad
Even glimpses of family life we have had.
We have loved all the babies,
The weddings, the fun
Had lovely street parties
And celebrated as one.
We are one great big family
And sure that you know
This land's admiration
Will just grow and grow.

AUDREY ALLOCCA

A GOLDEN JUBILEE

I'm travelling down from Aberdeen
To stop by in London and visit the Queen
I'm going to stop by for biscuits and tea
And give my best wishes for the grand Jubilee
Now sit back and hear the tale to be told
For having a Queen should never grow old
She had the crown placed upon her head
And it won't be passed on until she's officially dead
You'll always be reigning
From crowning till death
Thank you for your service to our country
Elizabeth
You're the head of the country
And your good works are seen
As we all stand united
Shouting, 'God save the Queen!'

MARY GALLAGHER

JUBILATIONS

Please Queen Elizabeth, don't look down
For 60 years you've been wearing that crown
You've worn so many outfits, shook so many hands
You've travelled to so many faraway lands
So many countries want you as their Queen
Think of the famous people you've seen
You've raised beautiful children, you've been a good wife
You should be proud of your Royal life

We've got days off school, we've made plans with friends
We're hoping the party just never ends
We've got bunting, games, music and fun
Fingers crossed we'll get some sun!
We've made all our flags, written stories and rhymes
We've learnt about Royals in olden times
The country will be wearing red, white and blue
It all for our Queen, Jubilations to you!

LEANNE BARRETT

JUBILEE MEMORIES

A photo of me, I'm aged only three,
Dressed up in red, white and blue,
My mum and my nan, behind us a man,
My grandpa in his best suit.
I'm twirling a flag, clasp sweets in a bag,
Cakes and pop in my belly,
The Queen, dressed in pink, my favourite I think,
A golden carriage on my telly.

Now my children wave and watch the parade,
Diamond now we celebrate.
My mum , my nan, but no longer a man,
My grandpa taken by age.
I take photographs of my children's laughs,
Celebrating and merry.
The Queen looks so grand, I hold my kids' hands;
The golden carriage on our telly.

J E ROWNEY

Ode To Her Majesty On Her 60th Jubilee

Your Royal Majesty
This year we celebrate your 60th Jubilee,
Your smile is alluring and quite disarming,
Thank you, for always being so charming!

You play a vital role,
You personify majesty deep within your soul.
During wartime, your nation was engulfed in grief –
Your sweet demeanour restored their shaken belief
In all that is good and right.
All through the years you never gave up the fight!

I love the way you persevere
Without displaying any fear,
In giving your all
You answered a nation's call.

The day you were crowned, what a beautiful sight!
Your people showed their utter delight!
A people's Queen –
Rarely has your equal been.

Your reign is a glorious one,
Elizabeth Regina, you have a great duty done!

Iris Ina Glatz

The Queen's Reign

Cast out the reign of our righteous Queen,
Encrusted with jewels she will wear again,
The crown for her Empire, a celebration awaits,
Let's joyfully cheer as she walks through the gates.

A welcoming presence she can expect,
Her patrons await her to pay their respects,
A gracious wave, an ambience of cheer,
For this is the Queen's Diamond Jubilee Year.

Suzelle Longman

Painting A Picture For The Queen

I've painted a picture for the Queen
I hope it isn't too obscene
I mean I hope she likes it
I've spent all night painting it.

While if I'm honest and don't get too big-headed
I think I've created a masterpiece
The colours are kind of psychedelic
But I'm hoping, with a bit of luck
She hasn't seen anything like it.

I wonder, will I get a medal
Or perhaps a title?
That would be nice
But then again, I'm not counting my chickens, not just yet.

While I've popped it in the post
And I reckon it's take a few days
To reach Buckingham Palace
And to her surprise
She'll be the first to set eyes on it.

Four weeks later; Mother have I got any post yet?
That's strange, I put the right address on the packet
Still no word
Am I a fool to think any different?

But to my surprise, when I least expected it
A letter did come in the post and in gold leaf letters
It said my painting is in her own private gallery
Imagine that, little old me
I think my dreams have been granted.

No longer am I blue
I can hold my head up proud
I painted a picture and now the world knows about it.

Clifford Heasley

JUBILEE MARCH

Par-rumpity-tum, par-rumpity-tum,
the band is playing par-rumpity-tum;
song of the trumpet and beat of the drum;
par-rumpity-tum, par-rumpity-tum.

She lives in a palace, she wears a crown,
when people meet her they bob up and down,
a little old lady, just like my mum
and the band is playing
rumpity-tum.

In big cars and golden coaches she goes,
magnificent robes and wonderful clothes
and those hats! only dreamt of by my mum!
and the band is playing
rumpity-tum.

Flags are a-fluttering, red, white and blue,
Folk are a-chattering, laughing crowds who
are waiting to see her; so is my mum!
They hear the band playing
rumpity-tum.

She's smiling and waving to left and right,
Wild cheers! though the pavement was hard last night!
They love her so much and so does my mum!
and the band is playing
rumpity-tum.

Why do we love her? Everyone knows
it's nothing to do with posh hats and clothes!
She's loyal and constant, just like my mum
while the band is playing
rumpity-tum.

She works very hard, never lets us down,
in countries abroad, in cities, in towns;
she must get so tired, like my poor mum!
but the band keeps playing
rumpity-tum.

So on she goes in her own special way,
serene and gracious and, day after day,
fulfilling her duties; just like my mum
'cause the band keeps playing
rumpity-tum.

And, just like my mum, she's been there all my life
and she has children and she is a wife
but because of that crown, her destiny,
she means something extra to you and me.

Today she is what she always has been,
our jewel, our Diamond Jubilee Queen;
amazing, priceless, spectacular and
the best in the history of this fair land.

Par-rumpity-tum, par-rumpity-tum,
Blow shining trumpet, beat loud festive drum!
Par-rumpity-tum, par-rumpity-tum
long may the band play on!
rumpity-tum.

VALERIE SUTTON

THE QUEEN'S DIAMOND JUBILEE

In June the Queen celebrates
Her Diamond Jubilee
She has a daughter, one and sons, three.
Elizabeth is the Queen to several countries
Sixteen states and twelve British colonies.
Queen Victoria celebrated her Diamond Jubilee
Being the only other Royal in history.
Children singing in a diamond choir
Around the world light beacons of fire.
With her husband, whom she joined in marriage
They travel from Westminster in a horse drawn carriage.
Her four heirs will join with her, for all the world to see
As she stands on the palace balcony.
People watching start to scream
'God save our gracious Queen.'

KAREN BROWN

DIAMOND JUBILEE

Graciousness is yours Ma'am;
You are noble in high courts.
Victorious we are, with you.

You are . . . within my thoughts . . .

God's breath upon this Kingdom.
Of Him you're not ashamed;
His glory is your service
And your calling to His name.

Thank you for your steadfastness
Through ugliness and pain;
A beacon for our homeland
Through your judicious reign.

Out of touch, yet so in touch . . .
Unreachable, yet reached.
Longer may you be our Queen
(A simple heart's beseech).

You've reached into each decade
With your father's humble glow;
Graced with your mother's tenets,
You're a credit to your vows.

BERYL ELIZABETH JUPP

THE QUEEN

To Your Royal Highness,
Its your special day,
It's your special year,
You have serviced the country for 60 years,
Not one day less,
So hold your head up high,
And the country will hold up a glass,
Time may have changed things,
You have seen a lot,
But you are still the same Royal Highness,
In our hearts you stay.

RACHEL MARTIN

OUR QUEEN

As iconic as
Fish and chips
Strawberries and cream
Welsh cakes
Cream tea
Princess Diana
Big Ben
Wimbledon
London Bridge
Windsor Castle
Buckingham Palace

Bunting will decorate the streets
Tables will line the roads
Chequered tablecloths
Balloons and party-poppers too.
Music playing in the street
What fun it will be
Fizzy pop
Sandwiches and cakes.
Children playing games
Laughter fills the air
'Hip hip hooray'
They'll cry.
Decked out
In their best outfits
Posies passed along to
The Queen
As she goes by
Everyone will cheer.

JESSICA STEPHANIE POWELL

TO QUEEN ELIZABETH ON HER DIAMOND JUBILEE

A diamond has many facets
And so indeed has been your reign
And dear Ma'am, we have surely seen
Your great joy and also your pain
Not affecting your work as our Queen
In family troubled waters
You have remained calm and steadfast
In your many Royal quarters

Yes, you are the glue which holds us
A much changed nation, together
Your servant-hood personified
However has blown the weather
As head of your family
You command the greatest respect
That you would like to escape sometimes
It is so easy to suspect!

Sixty years you have reigned for us
Quite devoid of desires for oneself
Devoted, humble, not without pain
Even surrounded by great wealth
From country to country travelling
Making journeys near and so far
Delighting all with your sunny smiles
And how lovely your outfits are!

The pinks, the blues and the yellows
For Ireland that emerald green
A tribute to healing division
Your purpose was so clearly seen
You came to the throne we realise
In the dawning of married life
With oh so little time to be a mother
And surely less to be a wife!

Walking with kings and commoners
You have touched the hearts of all men
In such a variety of roles
We have heard your quiet, 'Amen.'
So be it, for what you are called to do
And it's done with such perfection
And your people, Ma'am, you surely know
Hold you in great affection

Rich and poor have a warmth for you
Which pours from their every vein
We thank you for the glorious years
Sixty years of devoted reign
Heartfelt was your Christmas message
Heralding Jesus as Lord and King
Aware of our Christian heritage
Which many aside would have us fling

As you survey the weeping world
Disasters in every part
It's comforting to know
That |Jesus Christ is in your heart
We pray that, as your father did
You will call this nation to prayer
To prevent us falling into the abyss
To receive His protection and care

He or she who would valiant be
Let them proclaim the Word of God
To echo o'er our precious land
Where the saints before us have trod.
We cannot avoid the scriptures
Unfolding truths before our eyes,
And to add to them or deny them
Is the one who most surely dies!

And we thank God for your consort
So clearly an able support
We know he has been a comfort
As all husbands quite rightly ought!
Reign on, reign on, Your Majesty
In such compassion, truth and love
Being certain to take your orders
From King Jesus who reigns above.

PEARL COLEMAN

A Diamond Lady

Not long being married so it seemed,
So young and not quite ready,
Her duties since becoming our Queen,
Have now been long and steady,
Coronation parties set up in streets,
Folks did the best they could,
Televised so people could watch it,
Everything done properly by the book.

Six decades of time she has done us proud,
The good years outweighing the bad,
She always stands tall with head held high,
Even when we can tell she is sad,
Her grandchildren speak of her with pride,
In all she does her best,
We are lucky to have a Diamond Queen,
To us she will always be blessed.

So now it is her DIAMOND YEAR,
She must be feeling so proud,
All the people will be celebrating,
Flags waving and cheering out loud,
Congratulations to a special lady,
With Prince Philip by her side,
The smiles that beam across their faces,
Will be televised far and wide.

Elsie Kemp

Long To Reign Over Us

Not born to be a monarch, Elizabeth lived
a young life that was favoured and full.
Her parents, the Duke and Duchess of York
led lives which had never been dull.

She watched as her father supplanted a king
whose reign was decidedly short.
She helped many children survive the World War,
then married and formed her own court.

Elizabeth Alexandra Mary became our Queen
and is loved by us all.
She reigned with such insight and caring,
as soon as she answered that call.

So now, sixty years have gone by,
since in Kenya she heard she was Queen
and her father, George VI, had died in his sleep.
What an awakening that must have been.

But a woman of duty she turned out to be,
She followed her faithfulness through,
seeing countries at war and our military might.
Accepting the old and the new.

In June we will follow her steps to the coach
which carried her into our lives,
with Philip beside her, her consort so long,
our loyalty will never tire.

June Sharp

QUEENY

What you might not know about the Queen
Is that she is one big fighting machine,
Pictures may make you think otherwise
But I have trained and sneaky spies.
When lights are out and doors are locked
Queeny sneaks out to plan her plot
Spin down from a rope come the Queen spider
To steal the grandest tasting cider
Locked away with bolts is Queeny's best
1,000 pounds a bottle she'll have a fest
She grabs and snatches all in sight
Then spins back up into the dead of night
The sirens go, oh not again!
Queeny runs from the policemen
Bang and boom, all down they go
Her hat and purse, oh did she throw
Wait, wait, wait, this isn't right
I almost had a nervous fright
Wow, wow, wow this isn't our Queen
Or a big mean fighting machine.
Our Queen is red and white and blue
Because she will smile and laugh with you
And upon her arm is Prince Phil
And when with him she can chill
Her smile is pure as finest gold
And her dear purse she does hold
To her Corgis, what a bunch
I wonder how much do they munch?
For sixty years look how much she's done
What an individual one
From birth to her Coronation
Her beauty struck her loving nation.
Her diamond years have come at last
And thanks to all she shall have a blast
Now I can say congrats to Lizzy
For many more years as Queen she'll be busy.

Long live the Queen Congratulations
You are the best Diamond Queen in the world!

ISOBEL FURMSTON

OUR QUEEN ELIZABETH

We've been to Buckingham Palace
The Tower of London too,
We saw the Union Jack Flying
It was red, white and blue.

It would have been nice to see the Queen,
But sadly she wasn't there,
We would have bowed and curtsied
To show her that we care.

The Queen is married to Prince Philip,
Her family is important too,
There's Anne, Charles, Edward and Andrew
To name just a few.

She has reigned now for 60 years,
She's in her Jubilee year,
We love and admire her
And give her a great big cheer.

ASHLEY LETCH, IAN BANNISTER, RICHARD MANTLE, MICHAEL SUTTON,
MICHAEL BARRELL, BERNADETTE SCRAFTON & ALEX ROBERTS

A PROMISE KEPT

From princess free to grandmother beloved,
Pledged to serve her whole life, short or long.
With steadfast faith and duty nobly borne,
Full sixty years on Britain's lonely throne.

Constant as rock, a diamond living now,
Her shining vow through joy and pain upheld.
For people most, no other monarch known;
Elizabeth, the jewel in Britain's crown.

LYNN NICKERSON

DIAMOND JUBILEE, A STREET CELEBRATES

Our avenue: a climb, a bend,
The punctual masterpiece of a camellia,
A surprise waft of summer bells,
The frosty shriek of the moonlight owl.

Boulevard, bolt-hole, harbour, haven,
A clock tower rises on a tablecloth of fields;
The sway of a silent cedar
As it makes a lattice of the sky.

Growth, change –
A carousel of seasons!
A girl skips up the avenue, comes back a woman;
Removals, arrivals.

Snow fell and did a drought once parch us?
Nests fill and empty;
Loved ones not with us any more,
We miss their smile, their wisdom.

Tonight, on ancient Ridgeway,
We'll light a beacon,
Not, as of old, to warn of enemy approach,
But tribally still, in hope -
In celebration, enjoying together from those heights
The sprinkled diamonds of our city's lights,
The clustered communities
Silently on show for us.

And through that beacon's purifying flames
Let's chase away all doubts:
Together we can burnish anew our fellowship,
Feared dim by some;
Together let's forge now something strong, bright and new;
And let the distant, scattered neighbourhoods
Bear silent witness to this pledge –
And let that be our day's crowning moment!
And let that be
Our Jubilee!

TONY SCARFI

REGINA

She stands by her window view
and looks down on the crowd
can I be the one they want,
can I make my parents proud?

She walks the steps they walked before
She greets those in her care
Inclines a hand and shares a smile
She's shaking all the while

Her fingers trace her heavy crown
she thinks of the quarter gone
how young I was she almost says
how young I feel I am

She stares back at her vanity
and strings on her best pearls
remembers how things used to be
when Margaret and she were girls

She smiles and thinks how fast it's been
to greet the new millennium
to look on subjects who lived in peace
as they march to another war

Tracing a tender placed gold locket
caressing beloved and be-loved
heavy on heart as her dear depart
and she must continue to smile

Time passes fast now
the young are now old
and so much has changed here
since she last wore her gold

They still sit beside her
as she sits on her throne
and recalls how very much
her small country has grown

SHANNON BAXTER

IN ODE OF EDMUND

Paudrez!
        Sauvegarder.
You, noble lady
Novel nouvelle enterprise
Lapped by the Indian Oceans of soft time

You, heavy with the lives of hegemony
Bent low as lilacs under wine

Like dirt-hogs snuffling, truffles' shuffling –
down warren 'ole roots that wind like webs
tinkling bells on the spider's spine

Oh you veritable Regina –
Historic bride of what was an at once and will be forever mine!
How I long to regard you;
        (really I long to
        regard you)
mint-eyed, tarpic, dual-lipped splendour
Smelling of copper, or silver, or burnt-burnish tarnished lime –

What joys would it cost me
to peer inside your mind?

Unscrew you like a jam jar
And peer into you:
Cast-iron queen,
With mouth-tight, eyes-bright, fists clenched
To the shape of ripe clementines.

Once a year, at the head of the year,
At the ash-mile, heaped-pile, dogsbody who coddled
        molly
turn of the times,
You flicker with grateful rubies
And with tongues of speech sparkle a moving portrait
that inscribes the passage of time.
On our heads are perched flimsy paper hats,
they flutter like
wild birds knocking damp dust under cat flaps;
Whilst outside the cold evening covers crisp-clean streets
And vulgar men with accents sprawled Atlantic-wide
Infiltrate our television screens

(they do not wield their mouths like you or me,
eh, Queenie?)

But *Oh* Great Lady You,
You do not and have not and nor do you not
Nor n/ever (not) disclose,
What is rightfully yours, and mine.

You cannot be like me; nor inhabit me;
But you, who reek of thy glory,
thy kingdom oozy, powerful with glory,
Are this, to thyn own country,
And to mine own heart art thine.

SARAH LEE LIAN HAND

QUEEN ELIZABETH II

There was once a princess who loved horses and dogs and studied history;
Never did she imagine she would be queen of a land so full of tradition and mystery.
When her father sadly died, she received a crown and a title so grand,
Was then she realised, her life would not now be as planned!

There were 39 monarchs before and will probably be many more,
She knew she wanted to be the best queen ever to everyone, rich or poor.
She took on her role as Head of State and Nation along with that of wife and mother,
And has accomplished many milestones and historic firsts almost like none other.

The Queen is now almost 86 and has been happily married for 64
She has had many celebrations – silver, gold and more.
And now only the greatest celebration of all remains
It's time for the Diamond Jubilee of our Queen's reign!

There will be celebrations everywhere in Britain
With 100s of boats in the Thames Pageant and Big Luncheon.
We thank you dear Queen for all your hard work and dedication
You are quite an inspiration to us, a young generation!

MEGHNA NANDI (8)

The Queen's Diamond Jubilee

Hip hip hooray, it's the Queen's Jubilee today.
The Union flag and all the bunting and streamers
Are taken out as we all cheer and shout.
As we celebrate the Queen's sixty years on the throne.

To mark this special year why can't they bring our service men and women safe home?
I'm sure that would please the Nation,
To have our fighting troops in a home station.

May it be Catterick camp or even Purbright
To bring them home safe is that not right?
They are fighting a fierce war
And getting killed by score and score.

While in the homeland we shout and cheer the Queen,
Men and women are getting killed unseen.
So why can't they stop this bloody, awful war
And fight the threat of terrorism from reaching the Nation's shore?

The Queen is the head of our land and she is doing just fine and grand, but it's her troops
that are fighting on the front line in the name of Her Majesty,
It's a high killing crime.

Roy Muir

God Save The Queen

Crowned in glory,
The beginning of the story,
Sixty years upon the throne,
In a country I'm glad to call home.

The ups and downs of a magnificent reign,
Things will never be quite the same,
Seeing many leaders come and go,
The time is yours, the time is now.

Once in a lifetime
To come up with this rhyme,
Here's to the next sixty years,
Hear the crowds and their cheers.

Jonathan Luke Simms

YOUR MAJESTY ELIZABETH II IN YEAR 2012

In the winter of Your Majesty's life, surrounded by a lively, beautiful family,
who all added surprises and quality to an eventful and amazing life.
A wonderful celebration of sixty years in a demanding role,
has set the scene in many places this year.
There is magic in the details when selecting outfits and jewellery
for travelling and meeting an ocean of people from all over the globe,
there is magic in the details when giving a speech.
With natural ease Ma'am has managed all this
And guided PMs, family members and other Royals too.
Shown us how connectedness to God reinforces stability, trust, respect and faith,
served the populations with culture, traditions, religion and history.
Survived The Press' intrusion – exposure and 'life in the public eye'
an achievement in its own right, much more than I could bear.
We are many people, greatly humbled and full of admiration.
Wishing congratulations with the Diamond Jubilee.

SUSSI LASSEN

REGINA

A monochromic world when first the maid came to her throne.
Now colour bright envelops us, while she remains serene.
Pay homage to the one we come to worship as our own,
This tiny figure, elegant, assured, anointed sovereign.
Black, brown and white, red, white and blue, her people she inspires.
With lions rampant, couchant, harp, the standard that she bears
Aloft, for all her subjects in both near and distant shires,
The rock on which we've based our hopes for sixty glorious years.
Did ever monarch rule before with such a velvet glove?
Respect is due to she, as Queen, but love for herself.
Voices raised in harmony, our crowned head above;
Allegiance to Her Majesty from all her Commonwealth.
When you've shouted 'Rule Britannia' and you've sung, 'God Save The Queen',
To Lilibet, our lady fair, of ever regal mien.

ALAN WISEMAN

THE KING IS DEAD, LONG LIVE THE QUEEN

Living in a foreign country
It strikes them as quite absurd
That we still maintain a monarchy
A view held by many abroad

The cost to benefit ratio
Of keeping a civil list
Compared to an elected president
Is an opportunity missed

But that would have no sense of history
As it comes down through the ages
The role of continuity
And how it helped to make us

The face of party politics
At worst corrupt and rotten
Successive party leaders
Gone and best forgotten

Those who wear the crown
Enter into eternity
Privileged to influence what
We were, are and could be

JAMES TIERNEY

OUR DIAMOND QUEEN

60 years of Elizabeth our Queen
from the moment of accession
to today's apocalyptic scene,
she has walked this narrow path
with assurance – always serene,
her dignity leaves no one in doubt
she can show a way calmly,
no need to shout –
from marriages gone wrong
to calming a seething throng,
when Diana died she put away pride
to have grandsons by her side,
from Buckingham Palace
each year she proceeds
down to the Parliament building
to speak to government and peers,
setting down plans her government
have laid for the good of all,
holding everyone listening to her
in her dignified thrall,
so God bless and keep her
for as long as He can
Queen of England
And Lord of Man.

ELIZABETH ADAMS

DIAMOND MAJESTY

All black and white and grainy you were
in 1953,
as, bedecked in glittering black and white,
you walked in black and white stateliness
across our black and white screens.

Since then what blinding colour
has flashed across your life,
some of it too bright to bear!
Yet somehow you've survived;

and like a subtly sparkling diamond, like a constant, timeless star,
you've carried on, regardless,
quietly resplendent,
wisely enigmatic.

Hats off to you, Ma'am, we all say!
Your Majesty is magic.

EILEEN CAIGER GRAY

CELEBRATION

Our figurehead, the Queen
Prince Philip her rock
60 years on the throne
To celebrate we will flock
We will dance in the street
We will dance in the park
We will be celebrating
Long after dark
60 years of change
Seen sunshine and rainfall
But Her Royal Highness
Sticks by us all
You have held your banner high
So do it once again
For Queen Elizabeth II
Long may she reign

JENNIFER BOSWORTH

Our Queen

In front of the TV we gathered
A neighbour had kindly allowed
Our faces flushed with excitement
As we watched the gathering crowd

A sandwich and cakes on the sofa
And a mug of tea in our hand
With eager anticipation
We awaited the trumpeting band

Inside the abbey was stillness
As the crown was placed on her head
The weight of it posing discomfort
And the thoughts in her mind were of dread

Too young to reign over an empire
Too young to be burdened this way
But undaunted her strength and her courage
Were apparent to all on this day

She's reigned ever since with a passion
For duty and honour and truth
With her heart, her soul and compassion
Left firmly behind was her youth

Stalwart the man who's beside her
And ever the rock that she needs
His arm always there to protect her
Albeit in essence *she* leads

So we love her for what she's accomplished
And we're so proud of who she's become
Our Sovereign, our Queen and our mother
Of a nation who will never succumb

Be it famine or war or destruction
Her steadfast approach will endure
To a country who dares to invade us
Her arrows will fly straight and sure

Her armies will honour and love her
Raising her banner on high
Our Sovereign, our Queen and our mother
For whom many a soldier would die.

Phillippa Leslie-Benson

DIAMOND DAYS

Where were you in Jubilee June?
On the water? By the water, proud
as Gloriana tossed her oars,
in saturated salutation
to a radiant river queen?

Did you hang bunting all around,
your joie de vivre undiluted?
Did you wear a paper crown and
splash through puddles bearing plates,
brimming with assorted fancies?

Did you muster on The Mall
a sea of smiles, waving not
drowning? Or, more audacious,
did you picnic at the palace
and post photographs on Facebook?

From John O'Groats to Land's End
and in distant realms beyond our shores,
the rush of beacons' flares mantled
the spheres to celebrate the glorious reign
of our most gracious monarch.

MIRIAM SULHUNT

THE NATION'S BEST FRIEND

D edicated
I nspiring
A wesome
M ajestic
O riginal
N oble
D utiful
S overeign.

CLAIRE-LOUISE PRICE

DIAMONDS

Surely diamonds are forever –
For you are our infinate Queen,
Sixty years of grace and dignity –
When you have ruled supreme.

Just twenty-five when your reign began,
You seemed to take it in your stride,
Bringing a new Elizabethan age,
With 'Philip' always by your side.

Through world and family troubles,
To your anointed course so true,
Even the most staunch republicans –
Have respect and regard for you.

Presidents and Prime Ministers –
How soon they have come and gone,
Few would want your dire decisions –
Or to make them for so long.

For The Crown can weigh so heavy,
Many rely on things you do –
But undaunted by your duty –
You come smiling and waving through.

A Jubilee tour's exhausting,
Endless faces and places to see,
But with you leading at the helm –
A sound success it's sure to be.

You'll never know what retirement is –
That's a perk your subjects enjoy,
The monarch's lot is to carry on –
Your work is a lifetime employ.

So yes! Those diamonds are forever,
And long remembered you will be,
As a star that shone so brightly –
In the Royal dynasty!

KATHY JORDAN

SALUTE TO QUEEN ELIZABETH

One of the most powerful persons
On the planet is Queen Elizabeth the Second
'Long live the Queen', is the anthem song I sang in 1952, with a drum in hand
Earlier in the 40s I sang, God save our King, for her elegant father
WWII destroyed our family with bullets in my father
She, with the handsome Philip Mountbatten raised four children
These are Charles, Anne, Andrew and Edward
With her wisdom she brought the nation and
Commonwealth forward
She is the most popular monarch, well travelled all over the world
In all aspects of stress, be it Diana generated or not, her serenity is bold and pure as gold
Looking back I remember with schoolmates,
I made a giant illuminated crown that glowed in the dark
She was our 26-year-old monarch
The British Embassy provided us with movies
Of Shirley Temple and Charlie Chaplin
So much of entertainment and fireworks
As an old man I still remember these sweet memories
And know my brain still works
All the same, I wanted to see her and travelled to Windsor Castle
There she was so splendid with majestic dazzle
The mind of the gallant lady evident in her tidy
Toy room and books to show
All these moulded her to be the Queen of our hearts
I stand there in wonder, gazing at her and pinch myself to know
'It's not a dream, sweetheart, she's real.'

RETHUAL GILBERT

QUEEN ELIZABETH: SIXTY GLORIOUS YEARS

Our Queen, our Queen, Queen Elizabeth II,
What can one say, sixty glorious years
Never one to shrink from her duties
She carries out her duties with a sense
Of pride and honour

Always on time and in good spirits
At her public engagements,
And
Shakes hands with much graciousness.

Long may she reign.

EFUE AVOR

QUEEN OF DIAMONDS

The brightest gem in the nation's crown.
A monarch of sixty years renown.
Your facets shine out to all the world.
To where the Commonwealth flags are unfurled.
Inspiring women and spreading love.
With the strength of a lion and the peace of a dove.
We celebrate this, your Jubilee year.
With congratulations and a hearty cheer.

MARGARET EDGE

CORONATION DAY IMPRESSIONS

My father stood seven foot one
    And had four eyes, that day.
For dear life to his neck I clung
    As the vast crowd did sway.

High on my perch I remember
    The flags flapping, so clear;
The day as dark as December
    The crowd all in good cheer.

The cavalrymen clip-clopping;
    The road slick from the rain;
The crowd on each foot was hopping
    As into view she came.

Like a golden crab her carriage
    Scuttled up past us proles.
His hands, my ankles a marriage
    Tight as Siamese souls.

Oh, the excitement! The splendour!
    Plucked from obscurity
Was I when our dear Queen – yes *her!*
    Waved directly at me!

Too quick went by the caravan;
    Quieter now the horde.
The talk all of tiaras and
    Her smile so bright and broad.

All good things must come to an end,
    I heard my father say.
Back on The Mall I'm small again:
    The sky further away.

Six decades hence have ducked and dived
    Since that magical morn,
When a towering lad aged five
    Saw a new era dawn.

BERNARD DOOGAN

Jubilee 1

It's unfortunate
You are still
Here, but as
You are we
Might as well
Make the best
Of things and
Not do our
Best to go
Around upsetting
People, pissing
On the graves
Of those less
Fortunate
Than yourselves
Forgetting
Not forgetting
By whose grace
You are where
You are and
Why the people
Love you
Not for who
You are but
What you are
And while you
Ride and hunt
And your children
And grandchildren
Ski the slopes
Don't forget
About us,
Those whom you
Euphemistically
Tongue firmly
In your cheek
Call your people.

Leon Green

DEDICATED

How well I remember your youthful accession,
so very soon after you flew to Africa,
your father standing gaunt, frail, hatless,
perhaps in his heart he knew a final farewell.
We grieved with you at so early a burden,
thankful that you had Philip by your side.
How regal and lovely always in your full regalia,
yet happy with family in head scarf and boots.
Still smiling serenely though hands and feet must ache,
so many more visits ahead in Jubilee year,
Tired doubtless, but your people are cheering
'It's her, here she comes,
Ooh isn't she marvellous!'
Your family like tentacles
touch your farthest boundaries,
each, in their own way,
reflect your example.
Ma'am, we're proud of you,
no others share our treasure,
a wise, smiling dynamo,
recharged for the next job.
Some might say your life is privileged,
no domestic worries or chores . . .
Well Chum, just you try it!
A full life of service, a labour of love.

DI BAGSHAWE

$\mathcal{F}$ORWARD $\mathcal{P}$OETRY
$\mathcal{I}$NFORMATION

We hope you have enjoyed reading this book -
and that you will continue to enjoy it in the coming years.

If you like reading and writing poetry drop us a line, or
give us a call, and we'll send you a free information pack.

Alternatively if you would like to order
further copies of this book or any of our other titles,
then please give us a call or log onto our
website at www.forwardpoetry.co.uk

Forward Poetry Information
Remus House
Coltsfoot Drive
Peterborough
PE2 9BF
01733 890099